First published in Great Britain 1984 by Colour Library Books Ltd.
© Illustrations and text: Colour Library Books Ltd.,
    Guildford, Surrey, England.
Display and text filmsetting by Acesetters Ltd.,
    Richmond, Surrey, England.
Colour separations by Llovet S.A., Barcelona, Spain.
Printed and bound in Barcelona, Spain by Rieusset and G. Estella.
Edited by Sarah Jane Evans
Stylist: Sarah Whitelock
Coordination: Hanni Edmonds
ISBN 0 86283 223 3

Text by
Maureen McCall
Photography by
Peter Barry
Designed by
Philip Clucas
Produced by
Ted Smart and Gerald Hughes
Editorial Direction by
David Gibbon

**Previous page: Topside of Beef
(top), Silverside (Salted) (centre
left) and Top Rib Pot Roast
(bottom).**

MEAT DISHES

BHS

Contents

Introduction

For centuries mankind has been rearing animals for their meat.

The buying, preparation, carving and presenting of meat is a very complex subject. Knowing how to cook a particular cut of meat is very important, and I hope this book will add to your knowledge.

For the home cook, however knowledgeable, there is no substitute for buying good quality meat and finding a butcher you can trust who will advise you and select good carcasses and prepare them skilfully.

Meals, however informal, are a shared occasion and the old tradition of the head of the family carving the roast at the table adds to the sense of communion.

The best aids to carving are a sharp knife and a two-pronged carving fork. It is also useful to have a firm working surface and plenty of elbow room, as well as a carving platter or board.

I am sure you will find this book a useful aid to cooking meat and will refer to it again and again.

Beef

Chilli Beef

PREPARATION TIME: 30 minutes

COOKING TIME: 2 hours

675g (1½lb) minced beef
40g (1½oz) fat
1 medium onion, peeled and chopped
1 clove garlic, crushed
300ml (½ pint) stock
15ml (1 tblsp) flour
30ml (2 tblsp) chilli powder
2.5ml (½ tsp) oregano
1 bayleaf
Seasoning

Brown minced beef in hot fat. Remove to a casserole. Brown onion and garlic in remaining fat and add to meat. Pour in stock until just covered. Cover and cook in a slow oven, 150°C, 325°F, Gas Mark 2, for about 1 hour. Mix flour and chilli powder smoothly with a little stock or water and stir into casserole. Add red kidney beans if required. Add oregano, bayleaf and seasoning and continue cooking for a further 30 minutes-1 hour.

Southseas Meat Balls

PREPARATION TIME: 20 minutes

COOKING TIME: 10-20 minutes

450g (1lb) minced beef
1 egg, beaten
Seasoning
15ml (1 tblsp) oil
3 small shallots, chopped
15g (2 tblsp) flour
450g (1lb) pineapple chunks
15ml (1 tblsp) soy sauce
5ml (1 tsp) wine vinegar
½ green pepper, finely chopped
25g (1oz) blanched almonds

Blend the beef, egg and seasoning in a large bowl. Make the beef mixture into four flat balls, brush with oil and grill for 10-20 minutes. Keep warm. Heat the oil in a frying pan. Fry the shallots gently for 3 minutes. Take out. Stir in the flour and cook the roux for 3 minutes. Pour in the juice from the canned pineapple and bring to the boil, stirring. Add the soy sauce and vinegar. Season. Add the shallots,

pineapple chunks, green pepper and almonds. Place the meatballs in the pan and heat through, spooning the sauce over.

Steak Diane

PREPARATION TIME: 20 minutes

COOKING TIME: from 5-20 minutes

1 onion, finely chopped
50-70g (2-3oz) butter
4 thin slices of sirloin steak
Worcestershire sauce
Brandy (optional)

Fry the onion in butter for a few minutes until soft. Add the steak and cook on both sides. Add Worcestershire sauce and the brandy to the butter. Ignite, if wished, and pour over the steaks. Garnish with chopped parsley.

Meat Roll

PREPARATION TIME: 30 minutes

COOKING TIME: 1 hour 30 minutes

450g (1lb) minced meat
100g (4oz) suet, finely chopped
1 onion, finely chopped
50g (2oz) fresh breadcrumbs
Seasoning
25g (1oz) dripping
Meat stock

For Coating
Beaten egg
Dry breadcrumbs

Mix the meat, suet, onion, fresh breadcrumbs and seasoning. If necessary add a little egg to bind. Shape into a thick roll, moulding out any cracks. Brush over with egg and coat with the dry breadcrumbs. Grease a piece of

greaseproof paper with the dripping and wrap round the roll. Secure the ends and lay in a baking tin. Bake for 1¼-1½ hours at 220°C, 425°F, Gas Mark 7. Just before serving, brush over with a little meat stock.

Beef Stroganoff

PREPARATION TIME: 30 minutes

COOKING TIME: 50 minutes

670-900g (1½-2lb) lean beef, cut into long strips
100g (4oz) butter
15ml (1 tblsp) oil
Flour
2-3 onions, chopped
100g (4oz) mushrooms, sliced
45ml (3 tblsp) dry sherry
300-450ml (½-¾ pint) stock
Seasoning
200ml (6 fl oz) sour cream

Melt butter in an oiled frying pan. Dip the strips of meat into seasoned flour and fry for several minutes. Transfer meat to a casserole. Fry onions for 7-10 minutes in the same fat. Spread over meat in casserole. Fry mushrooms for a few minutes. Add to casserole. Moisten with sherry and stock. Adjust seasoning to taste. Cover casserole and place in a slow oven, 170°C, 325°F, Gas Mark 2, for 30 minutes or until meat is tender. Add sour cream and cover again until heated through.

This page: Southseas Meat Balls (top right), Chilli Beef (centre left) and Meat Roll (bottom).

Facing page: Steak Diane (top), Beef Stroganoff (centre) and Steak and Kidney Pudding (bottom).

Roasted Fore Rib

PREPARATION TIME: 20 minutes

COOKING TIME: 15 minutes per 450g (1lb), plus 15 minutes

Place meat in a roasting tin and spread with dripping or cooking fat and season. Place in the centre of a preheated oven 180°C, 350°F, Gas Mark 4. If a covered roasting tin is used, basting is not necessary, but if the joint is uncovered the meat should be basted every 20-30 minutes. The meat should be turned over, using 2 metal spoons, halfway through the cooking. When the meat is cooked, transfer to a large carving dish. Keep hot.

Meat Roll in Pastry Case

PREPARATION TIME: 45 minutes

COOKING TIME: 30 minutes

450g (1lb) minced meat
1 onion, finely minced
100g (4oz) suet, finely chopped
Seasoning
225g (8oz) shortcrust pastry
Egg or milk to glaze

Fry mince and onion till cooked. Remove from pan. Mix the meat, suet, onion and seasoning together. If necessary add a little egg to bind to a pliable, slightly moist, mixture. Shape into a thick roll, moulding out any cracks. Roll out a piece of pastry large enough to cover the roll. Brush with egg or milk to glaze. Lay meat roll in a loaf tin and cook at 200°C, 400°F, Gas Mark 6, for about 20 minutes until pastry is golden brown.

Silverside (Salted)

PREPARATION TIME: soak overnight

COOKING TIME: 20 minutes per 450g (1lb) plus 20 minutes

To prepare meat for cooking, soak meat overnight in cold water to remove excess salt. Put the joint into a pan and cover with cold water. Bring to the boil, then pour off the liquor. Cover again with cold water and bring to the boil. After 5 minutes, reduce the heat and allow to simmer for the appropriate length of time.

Meat Roll in Pastry Case (far left), Curried Shepherd's Pie (top centre), Roasted Fore Rib (bottom centre) and Monday Beef Casserole (bottom right).

Curried Shepherd's Pie

PREPARATION TIME: 20 minutes

COOKING TIME: 45 minutes

350g (12oz) minced beef
2 onions, finely chopped
25g (1oz) fat
15g (½oz) flour
15ml (1 tblsp) curry powder
300ml (½ pint) stock or a small tin
    of tomatoes and a little stock
Seasoning
15ml (1 tblsp) chutney
450g (1lb) mashed potatoes

Fry onions in hot fat. Add flour and curry powder. Add stock or tomatoes and stock. Bring to the boil and cook until thickened. Add the minced beef and cook gently, stirring from time to time. Break up any lumps in the mince. Add seasoning and chutney. When meat is tender put into a pie dish. Cover with the mashed potatoes. Brown in oven or under grill until crisp.

Beef Cobbler

PREPARATION TIME: 45 minutes

COOKING TIME: 2 hours
15 minutes

Stew
50g (2oz) fat
2 large onions, sliced
750g (1½lb) stewing steak, diced
15ml (1 tblsp) paprika
150ml (¼ pint) water
1 green pepper, seeded, cored and
   diced
4 tomatoes, skinned and quartered
Seasoning

Cobbler
175g (6oz) self-raising flour
Seasoning
40g (1½oz) margarine
Milk

Stew
Heat fat and fry the onions and
diced meat until brown. Stir in
paprika, blended with water, and
the rest of the ingredients. Put into
a covered casserole and cook for
2¼ hours at 150-170°C, 300-
325°F, Gas Mark 2-3.

Cobbler
Sieve dry ingredients, rub in
margarine and mix to a soft dough
with milk. Cut into small rounds
and put on top of beef mixture.
Glaze with a little milk. Turn oven
up to 220°C, 425°F, Gas Mark 7,
until cobbler mixture is golden
brown.

Monday Beef Casserole

PREPARATION TIME: 25 minutes

COOKING TIME: 10-20 minutes

2 cups mashed potato
1 egg, beaten
1.25ml (¼ tsp) salt
175g (6oz) cooked beef, chopped
½ cup celery, chopped
100g (4oz) milk
Salt to taste
Dash nutmeg
Margarine or butter

Beat potatoes with egg and salt. Put
half the potatoes in the bottom of a
greased casserole. Blend and add
remaining ingredients, except
butter, to casserole. Cover with
remaining potatoes. Dot with
butter and bake in oven at 190°C,
375°F, Gas Mark 5, until top is
browned.

Topside of Beef

PREPARATION TIME: 5 minutes

COOKING TIME: 15 minutes per
450g (1lb) plus 15 minutes

Place meat in a roasting tin and
spread with dripping or cooking fat
and season. Place in the centre of a
preheated oven at 180°C, 350°F,
Gas Mark 4. If a covered roasting
tin is used basting is not necessary.
If the joint is uncovered, the meat
should be basted every 20-30
minutes. The meat should be
turned over, using two metal
spoons, halfway through the
cooking. When the meat is cooked,
transfer to a large carving dish and
keep hot.

Steak and Kidney Pudding

PREPARATION TIME: 30 minutes

COOKING TIME: 4 hours

675g (1½lb) stewing steak
2 lamb's kidneys
15ml (1 tblsp) flour
Seasoning
350g (12oz) suet crust pastry
150ml (¼ pint) stock

Cut steak and kidney into cubes
and mix together. Put flour and
seasoning onto a plate and toss
meat in this. Line a pudding basin
with the pastry. Put in meat, add
enough stock to come two-thirds
of the way up the basin. Roll out
remaining pastry to make a lid and
place on top of basin. Cover with
greased paper. Fix firmly round the
basin rim. Put the basin in a
steamer. Stand this over a saucepan
of boiling water. Steam for 4 hours.
Allow water to boil rapidly for the
first 2 hours, add more boiling
water when necessary.

Steak Pie

PREPARATION TIME: 30 minutes

COOKING TIME: 2 hours
15 minutes

750g (1½lb) stewing steak
40g (1½oz) flour
Seasoning
50g (2oz) fat
2 onions, sliced and chopped

600ml (1 pint) brown stock
225g (8oz) flaky pastry

Prepare the steak, cutting it into
pieces. Roll in seasoned flour and
fry in hot fat for a few minutes in a
saucepan. Add onions and turn in
the fat for 2-3 minutes. Stir in the
stock gradually, bring to the boil
and cook until the sauce has
thickened. Then lower the heat
and simmer for 1½ hours. Put the
steak into a pie dish. Roll out the
pastry. Put a band of pastry round
the moistened rim of the pie dish.
Top with the rest of the pastry, seal
the edges. Bake for 40-45 minutes
at 230°C, 450°F, Gas Mark 8.

Swiss Steak

PREPARATION TIME: 25 minutes

COOKING TIME: 1 hour
30 minutes

450-670g (1-1½lb) thick slice of
   steak
15ml (1 tblsp) plain flour
Seasoning
Dripping or margarine
1 medium tin peeled tomatoes
1 onion, peeled and grated

Mix flour and seasoning together
and rub well into the surface of the
meat. Melt dripping in a saucepan
and fry meat gently until brown.
Rub tomatoes through a sieve and
add to meat with grated onion.
Place joint, onions and tomatoes in
a casserole dish. Cover and simmer
gently at 180°C, 350°F, Gas Mark
4, for 1½ hours.

Top Rib Pot Roast

PREPARATION TIME: 25 minutes

COOKING TIME: 30 minutes per
450g (1lb)

50g (2oz) good dripping
6 large onions, peeled
6 large carrots, peeled
3 large turnips, peeled
1-1.5kg (2-3lb) piece of top rib,
   boned and rolled
Seasoning

Melt dripping in a large pan and fry
vegetables until a good brown
colour, then take out of pan. Fry
meat on all sides over a fierce heat
to seal in juices. Return vegetables
to pan, with just enough water to
give about 3½cm (1½ inches) in

depth. Season well. Put meat on
top of vegetables and cover pan.
The vegetables should not be too
small, otherwise they may break
during cooking. Reduce heat so the
liquid simmers gently. Carve the
meat as you would a roast joint.
The liquid from the pan can be
used for the gravy.

Stew and Dumplings

PREPARATION TIME: 30 minutes

COOKING TIME: 2 hours
20 minutes

500-750g (1-1½lb) beef steak
Seasoning
40g (1½oz) fat
2 onions, sliced
2 or 3 large carrots, sliced
450ml (¾ pint) water
½ bayleaf
Mixed herbs

For Dumplings
100g (4oz) self-raising flour
Seasoning
50g (2oz) shredded suet
Water to mix

Cut the meat into cubes, season,
then brown in the fat. Add onions,
carrots, water and herbs. Cover
pan and cook slowly for 2 hours.

For Dumplings
Sieve the dry ingredients together,
add the suet and mix to a dough
with the water. Roll into balls with
lightly-floured hands. Check there
is sufficient liquid in the stew, then
drop in the dumplings and cook for
15-20 minutes.

**Facing page: Steak Pie (top),
Beef Cobbler (centre left) and
Stew and Dumplings (bottom
right).**

Peppered Steak

PREPARATION TIME: 15 minutes

COOKING TIME: from
5-25 minutes

4 rump or fillet steaks
Oil
30ml (2 tblsp) black hot peppers for
    steak
50g (2oz) butter
Salt
60ml (4 tblsp) brandy
45ml (3 tblsp) single cream
Watercress

Brush the steaks on both sides with oil, then coat with black hot peppers and crush into the steak with a steak hammer. Melt butter in a frying pan and cook steaks for about 1½ minutes on each side. Reduce heat and cook for about a further minute (for rare steak), 3 minutes (for medium steak) or 7 minutes (if a well-done steak is required). Season with salt. Warm brandy in a ladle near the heat. Set it alight and pour over steaks. Remove steaks and place on a warmed serving dish. Keep hot. Stir cream into the juices in the frying pan. Heat gently for a few minutes. Pour sauce over steaks and garnish with watercress.

Steak Française

PREPARATION TIME: 30 minutes

COOKING TIME: 30-40 minutes

450-750g (1-1¼lb) rump steak
Seasoning
45ml (3 tblsp) Pernod
2 onions, peeled and chopped
450g (1lb) tomatoes, skinned and
    chopped
25g (1oz) butter
2.5ml (½ tsp) marjoram

Cut steak into 1cm (½ inch) strips with a sharp knife. Place in a shallow dish. Sprinkle with seasoning and Pernod. Cover and

Steak Française (left), Peppered Steak (centre) and Beef in Cider (right).

leave on one side for 1 hour. Fry onions in melted butter until tender but not brown. Add tomatoes and stir well. Add onions and tomatoes to the steak mixture with the marjoram. Cook in an oven just above the centre at 180°C, 350°F, Gas Mark 4, for 30-40 minutes.

Beef in Cider

PREPARATION TIME: 30 minutes

COOKING TIME: 2 hours 30 minutes

450g (1lb) blade steak
25g (1oz) fat
3 medium onions, quartered
4 carrots, quartered
1 clove garlic, crushed
225g (8oz) tomatoes, sliced
Seasoning
600ml (1 pint) dry cider

Cut beef into cubes and brown lightly in fat. Brown the onions and carrots. Put meat into an overproof dish with onions, carrots, garlic and tomatoes. Add seasoning to taste and cover with cider. Put on lid and cook at 170°C, 325°F, Gas Mark 3, for 2½ hours.

Goulash

PREPARATION TIME: 25 minutes

COOKING TIME: 2 hours

675g (1½lb) stewing steak
25g (1oz) fat
2 onions, peeled and chopped
2 carrots, peeled and chopped
25g (1oz) flour
1 beef stock cube
45ml (3 tblsp) tomato purée
450ml (¾ pint) water
10ml (2 tsp) paprika
45ml (3 tblsp) yogurt

Cut meat into cubes and brown in hot fat. Remove to a casserole dish. Put onions and carrots into a pan and fry until lightly browned. Add to meat. Put flour, crumbled stock cube and tomato purée into pan and add a little more fat if necessary. Cook for a few minutes, then add paprika and water and stir until boiling. Pour into casserole, cover and cook in a slow oven, 150°C, 300°F, Gas Mark 2, for about 2 hours. Just before serving, adjust seasoning and stir in yogurt.

Beefburgers

PREPARATION TIME: 25 minutes

COOKING TIME: 10-20 minutes

1 large onion, finely chopped
450g (1lb) minced beef
45ml (3 tblsp) fresh breadcrumbs
60ml (4 tblsp) milk
Salt
Paprika
5ml (1 tsp) mustard powder
Oil
4 burger buns, sliced horizontally
4 tomatoes, sliced (optional)
4 slices of Cheddar cheese (optional)

Preheat the grill. Mix the onion, minced beef, breadcrumbs and milk in a large bowl. Season with salt, paprika and mustard. Leave for 10 minutes. Make four beefburgers from the mixture. Brush with oil. Cook for 5 minutes on both sides under the grill. Remove from heat. Top the burgers with tomato and cheese, if desired. Put back under the grill to melt cheese. Serve in warm buns.

Grilled Fillet Steak

PREPARATION TIME: 10 minutes

COOKING TIME: from 5-20 minutes .

Fillet steak
Butter or oil

Preheat grill. Put steak on the grid of the grill pan and brush with melted butter or oil. Cook on one side, then turn over with tongs. Brush second side with butter or oil. Minute steak – 1 minute cooking each side. Under-done steak (rare) (¾ inch thick), 3-4 minutes. Medium-done steak – cook as under-done, then cook under lower heat for a further 3 minutes. Well-done steak – cook as under-done, then cook under lower heat for further 5-6 minutes.

Sausage and Egg Flan

PREPARATION TIME: 20 minutes

COOKING TIME: 30-40 minutes

175g (6oz) shortcrust pastry
450g (1lb) beef sausages
2 eggs
150ml (¼ pint) milk
1.25ml (¼ tsp) made mustard

Roll out pastry to line a deep flan case and prick the base. Fry sausages until cooked. Place in flan case. Whisk eggs. Add milk and mustard. Pour whisked mixture over the sausages. Place flan in oven, 230°C, 440°F, Gas Mark 8, for 15 minutes. Reduce temperature to 170°C, 325°F, Gas Mark 3, for a further 30 minutes, until pastry is cooked.

Cinnamon Roast

PREPARATION TIME: 30 minutes

COOKING TIME: 2 hours 30 minutes

1.5-2kg (3-4lb) brisket of beef
25g (1oz) flour
Seasoning
5ml (1 tsp) powdered cinnamon
25g (1oz) dripping
3-4 carrots, peeled and chopped
1 bayleaf
450ml (¾ pint) stock
1 onion

Coat joint with flour, seasoning and cinnamon. Melt fat in a pan and brown joint all over. Transfer joint to a dish. Fry onion and carrot until soft in the pan. Replace joint on top of vegetables. Put in bayleaf and add stock. Cover and simmer gently for 2-2½ hours. Thicken liquor with flour and serve separately.

This page: Cinnamon Roast (top), Curried Chuck Steak (centre left) and Swiss Steak (bottom right).

Facing page: Beefburgers (top left), Sliced Cold Beef and Bubble and Squeak (top right) and Grilled Fillet Steak (bottom).

Sausages in Tomato Sauce

PREPARATION TIME: 20 minutes
COOKING TIME: 25 minutes

450g (1lb) beef sausages
3 sticks celery, sliced
50g (2oz) salted peanuts

Tomato Sauce
15g (½oz) margarine
2 onions, finely chopped
2 carrots, finely chopped
1 stick celery, finely chopped
15g (½oz) flour
25g (1oz) tomato paste
50g (2oz) chopped red pepper
1 chicken stock cube
300ml (½ pint) boiling water
1 clove garlic, crushed
½ bayleaf
Sprig thyme
Seasoning
45ml (3 tblsp) medium sherry

Tomato Sauce
Put the margarine in a saucepan, add the onions, carrots and celery and brown slightly. Add the flour, stir and brown slightly, until the flour is sandy in colour. Add the tomato paste and red pepper. Stir well. Cool. Add the stock cube mixed with the boiling water, add garlic and herbs. Season and simmer for 1 hour, then check the seasoning. Sieve the sauce and stir in the sherry.

Sausages
Grill the sausages and keep them hot in a dish. Scald the celery sticks for 5 minutes in boiling water. Drain and add to the sausages. Pour the sauce over and keep hot. When ready to serve, garnish with salted peanuts.

Sliced Cold Beef and Bubble and Squeak

PREPARATION TIME: 20 minutes
COOKING TIME: 10-20 minutes

Sliced cold beef enough for 4 servings
½ medium cabbage
40g (1½oz) butter
1 small onion, finely chopped
Leftover mashed potato equal to the amount of cabbage

Bring a saucepan of water to the boil. Remove the core and any damaged leaves from the cabbage. Shred the cabbage. Put the cabbage into the water and cook for 6-7 minutes. Drain well. Heat the butter in a large frying pan. Fry the

onion gently until softened. Add the cabbage and stir over a low heat for 2 minutes. Fold in the mashed potato until it is completely mixed with the cabbage. Press the mixture lightly into the frying pan to form a large pancake. Cook for 5 minutes or until the underside is lightly browned. Turn and brown on the other side for 5 minutes. Serve very hot with the sliced cold meat.

Curried Chuck Steak

PREPARATION TIME: 35 minutes

COOKING TIME: 3 hours

750g (1¼lb) chuck steak, cut and diced
25g (1oz) fat
1 large onion, chopped
15-30ml (1-2 tblsp) curry powder
15ml (1 tblsp) paprika
50g (2oz) walnuts
50g (2oz) blanched almonds
25g (1oz) flour
450ml (¾ pint) stock
Seasoning
50g (2oz) desiccated coconut
50g (2oz) sultanas
15ml (1 tblsp) redcurrant jelly
15ml (1 tblsp) lemon juice
50g (2oz) mixed spice

Melt the fat and fry meat and onion until just brown. Add curry powder, paprika, walnuts and almonds and cook for 3 minutes. Stir in flour and cook gently for several minutes. Gradually blend in stock. Bring to boil and cook until thickened. Season and add coconut, sultanas, redcurrant jelly and lemon juice. Transfer mixture to a casserole, cover and cook at 170°C, 325°F, Gas Mark 3, for 2½-3 hours.

Sausage and Egg Flan (far left), Sausages in Tomato Sauce (bottom centre) and Goulash (top right).

Lamb

COOKING TIME: 2 hours

1kg (2lb) best end of neck of lamb
225g (8oz) onions, peeled and
    chopped
450g (1lb) carrots, peeled and
    chopped
750g (1½lb) potatoes, peeled and
    thickly sliced
Seasoning
2.5ml (½ tsp) dried thyme
900ml (1½ pints) boiling water
Chopped parsley

Cut neck into chops and season
well. Put alternating layers of
vegetables and meat in a large
casserole dish. Season well between
the layers and sprinkle the herbs at
the same time. Finish with a layer
of potatoes. Pour the water over
the meat, cover and cook in a slow
oven 170°C, 325°F, Gas Mark 3,
for about 2 hours. Just before
serving, skim and sprinkle well with
parsley.

Roast Herbed Leg of Mutton

PREPARATION TIME: 15 minutes

COOKING TIME: 30 minutes per
450g (1lb) plus 30 minutes

1 leg mutton
2-3 cloves garlic
2 bayleaves
100g (4oz) soft butter
225g (8oz) fresh breadcrumbs
5ml (1 tsp) thyme
5ml (1 tsp) rosemary
15ml (1 tblsp) chopped parsley
Juice of ½ lemon
Seasoning

Prepare a sheet of foil to wrap meat
completely. Slice 1 or 2 of the garlic
cloves and insert in small cuts on

Festive Leg of Lamb

PREPARATION TIME: 30 minutes

COOKING TIME: 30-35 minutes
                        per 450g (1lb)

1 leg of lamb
225g (8oz) pineapple rings
Glacé cherries

Score the surface of the joint in a
diamond pattern. Drain the
pineapple and reserve the juice.
Place the joint in a roasting tin and
pour the pineapple juice over the
scored surface. Roast at 180°C,
350°F, Gas Mark 4, basting
occasionally. Cut pineapple rings in
half. Garnish the joint with pieces
of pineapple in a line down the

length of the leg. Pin each piece in
place with a cherry on a cocktail
stick and serve.

Country Lamb Casserole

PREPARATION TIME: 30 minutes

**This page: Roast Lamb with
Rosemary (top right), Savoury
Pudding (top left) and Lamb
Kebab (bottom).**

**Facing page: Country Lamb
Casserole (top left), Wagon
Wheel Lamb (top right) and
Roast Herbed Leg of Mutton
(bottom).**

underside of meat. Place meat on foil, with bayleaves underneath. Cream butter with rest of the ingredients and crushed garlic cloves. Spread over the surface of the meat. Cover with foil and roast in the centre of the oven at 200°C, 400°F, Gas Mark 6. Then uncover and baste with the butter that has run onto foil. Continue roasting, uncovered, for 30 minutes, until crust is brown and crisp.

Lancashire Hot Pot

PREPARATION TIME: 45 minutes

COOKING TIME: 2 hours 30 minutes

450g (1lb) middle or best end of neck, cut into cutlets
15ml (1 tblsp) seasoned flour
4 medium onions, sliced
2 lamb's kidneys, skinned, cored and sliced
225g (½lb) mushrooms, sliced
675g (1½lb) potatoes, sliced
450ml (¾ pint) stock
Chopped parsley

Trim the lamb of any excess fat and coat with seasoned flour. Place layers of lamb, onion, kidney, mushrooms and potatoes in a large casserole, finishing with a layer of potatoes. Add the stock, cover and bake in a moderate oven, 180°C, 350°F, Gas Mark 4, for 2 hours. Remove the lid and cook for a further ½ hour to brown the potatoes. Sprinkle with chopped parsley.

Lemon and Ginger Chops

PREPARATION TIME: 3 hours

COOKING TIME: 15 minutes

4 chump lamb chops

Marinade
60ml (4 tblsp) oil
Grated rind of 1 lemon
30ml (2 tblsp) lemon juice
15ml (1 tblsp) ground ginger
Seasoning

Mix all the marinade ingredients together. Place the chops in a shallow dish and pour the marinade over them. Leave for 2-3 hours, turning occasionally. Remove the chops and place under a hot grill for 15 minutes, turning the chops occasionally and basting them with the marinade. Serve at once.

Wagon Wheel Lamb

PREPARATION TIME: 30 minutes

COOKING TIME: 20 minutes per 450g (1lb)

1-1.5kg (2-2½lb) loin or best end of neck of lamb
25g (1oz) fat
Small tin pineapple rings, cut in halves
10-20ml (2-4 tsp) brown sugar
Juice of ½ lemon

Garnish
175g (6oz) wagon wheel pasta
1.5 litres (3 pints) water
Salt
25-50g (1-2oz) butter

Place meat into a roasting tin and brush lightly with melted fat. Roast for 20 minutes per 450g (1lb) at 220°C, 425°F, Gas Mark 7. 30 minutes before end of cooking time, remove joint from oven and make six slits in the fat and skin. Press one pineapple half into each slit, brush with melted fat. Return to oven for rest of cooking time. When cooking time is finished, place the meat onto a hot dish and pour off all but 15ml (1 tblsp) of the fat.

Garnish
Chop the rest of the pineapple, add to the fat with the pineapple syrup, sugar and lemon juice, and heat. Cook pasta in boiling, salted water, strain and toss in butter. Arrange pasta around the meat and serve the syrup in a sauceboat.

Roast Lamb with Rosemary

PREPARATION TIME: 20 minutes

COOKING TIME: 20 minutes per 450g (1lb) plus 20 minutes

½ leg lamb
50g (2oz) butter
Seasoning
Rosemary
1 clove garlic (optional)
1kg (2lb) potatoes, peeled and cut into thick slices

Spread butter over lamb and season well. Stick rosemary leaves into the fat of the meat. Insert a clove of garlic near the bone. Place joint on a rack in a roasting tin. Roast in the centre of the oven at 220°C, 425°F, Gas Mark 7. Place sliced potatoes under the meat after it has been cooking for 30 minutes. Baste joint from time to time.

Lamb Kebab

PREPARATION TIME: 15 minutes

COOKING TIME: 10-25 minutes

350g (¾lb) lean lamb, cut into bite-size pieces
450g (1lb) chipolata sausages, cut into halves
4 small tomatoes, halved or quartered

Thread a mixture of the lamb, tomatoes and sausages onto metal skewers. Brush with melted butter and cook under the grill, turning the skewers to make sure that the food is well cooked.

Cutlets and Tomato Dip

PREPARATION TIME: 30 minutes

COOKING TIME: 30-45 minutes

4 large or 8 small cutlets
1 egg, beaten
45ml (3 tblsp) crisp breadcrumbs
Fat for frying

For the Dip
1 medium onion, peeled and chopped
1 small apple, peeled and chopped
25g (1oz) butter or margarine
Small tin or tube tomato purée
5ml (1 tsp) cornflour
300ml (½ pint) water
Seasoning
Pinch sugar
Pinch garlic salt

Coat cutlets with beaten egg and breadcrumbs. Fry onions and apple in the hot butter for several minutes. Add the tomato purée and cornflour blended with the water. Bring the mixture to the boil and cook steadily, stirring well until it comes to the boil and thickens slightly. Add the rest of the ingredients, lower the heat and continue cooking until a thick dip is made. Fry the cutlets in hot fat until golden brown and drain on kitchen paper. Serve with the tomato dip.

Rolled and Stuffed Breast of Lamb

PREPARATION TIME: 15 minutes

COOKING TIME: 25 minutes per 450g (1lb) plus 25 minutes

900g (2lb) breast of lamb, boned
Sage and onion stuffing
A little oil or fat
Seasoning

Spread the breast of lamb with stuffing and roll. Brush the lamb with oil or melted fat. Season. Allow 25 minutes per 450g (1lb) + 25 minutes cooking time – weigh after stuffing meat. Place in roasting tin and cook at 170°C, 325°F, Gas Mark 3.

Lancashire Hot Pot (top right), and Cutlets and Tomato Dip (above right) and Lemon and Ginger Chops (bottom right).

Stuffed Lamb Chops

PREPARATION TIME: 40 minutes

COOKING TIME: 35 minutes

4 chump lamb chops

Stuffing
1 small onion, finely chopped
25g (1oz) butter
2 lamb's kidneys, skinned, cored and chopped
50g (2oz) mushrooms, chopped
25g (1oz) fresh breadcrumbs
15ml (1 tblsp) sherry
1 tsp chopped parsley
Seasoning
10ml (2 tsp) oil or melted fat

Garnish
50g (2oz) button mushrooms
2 small tomatoes, halved
Triangle of bread
Parsley
A little oil or fat

Using a sharp knife, cut each chop horizontally through the fat and meat to make a small pocket for stuffing.

Stuffing
Fry the onion in butter, add the kidneys and mushrooms and continue cooking gently for 5 minutes. Add the rest of the ingredients and mix well. Press a spoonful of the stuffing into the pocket of the chops. Brush chops with oil. Grill the chops under a medium heat for 8-10 minutes on each side, turning once, until cooked.

Garnish
Fry the button mushrooms, tomatoes and bread. Serve the chops on a hot dish garnished with the tomatoes, mushrooms and triangles of bread.

Lamb Chops and Mint Sauce

PREPARATION TIME: 10 minutes

COOKING TIME: 25 minutes

4 lamb chops

Mint Sauce
30ml (2 tblsp) mint leaves
10ml (2 tsp) sugar
30ml (2 tblsp) vinegar
7.5ml (½ tblsp) hot water

Grill chops until cooked and tender. Keep hot. Wash and dry

the mint leaves. Place on a chopping board with 5ml (1 tsp) sugar. Chop until fine, then put into a sauceboat. Add the rest of the sugar, stir in the hot water and leave for a few minutes to dissolve sugar. Add the vinegar. Serve with the chops.

Moussaka

PREPARATION TIME: 45 minutes

COOKING TIME: 1 hour 20 minutes

450g (1lb) aubergines, thinly sliced
15g (½oz) oil
2 large onions, thinly sliced
1 clove garlic, crushed
450g (1lb) minced lamb
425g (15oz) tin tomatoes
30ml (2 tblsp) tomato purée
Seasoning
2 eggs
150g (5oz) single cream
50g (2oz) Cheddar cheese, grated
25g (1oz) Parmesan cheese, grated

Fry the aubergines in oil for 3-4 minutes. Remove and drain well. Fry the onions and garlic in 15ml

(1 tblsp) oil until golden brown. Add the lamb and cook for about 10 minutes, stirring occasionally. Add the tomatoes and tomato purée. Mix well. Bring to the boil and simmer for 20-25 minutes, season. Arrange alternate layers of aubergines and the lamb mixture in a large soufflé dish or shallow casserole dish. Bake in oven, 180°C, 350°F, Gas Mark 4 for 35-40 minutes. Beat the eggs and cream together and stir in the cheese. Pour onto the moussaka and return to the oven for a further 15-20 minutes until the top is firm and golden brown.

Lamb and Kidney Pie

PREPARATION TIME: 50 minutes

COOKING TIME: 2 hours

1 large onion, thinly sliced
30ml (2 tblsp) oil
450g (1lb) lamb from leg or shoulder, cubed
15ml (1 tblsp) flour
225g (8oz) lamb's kidney, skinned, cored and chopped

100g (4oz) mushrooms, sliced
150ml (¼ pint) beef stock or red wine
Few drops of gravy browning
Seasoning
200g (7oz) packet frozen pastry, thawed
Beaten egg to glaze

Fry the onion in oil until soft, but not brown. Toss the lamb in the flour with the kidney. Add to the onion and fry for 5-10 minutes, stirring occasionally. Add the mushrooms, stock, gravy browning and seasoning. Bring to the boil, stirring. Cover and simmer for 1 hour. Cool. Transfer the lamb mixture to a pie dish, then roll out the pastry. First make a collar of pastry round the dish and cover the pie. Seal edges but make a small hole in centre to allow the steam to escape. Brush with beaten egg to glaze. Cook at 220°C, 425°F, Gas Mark 7, for 10-15 minutes. Reduce the heat to 190°C, 375°F, Gas Mark 5, for a further 25-30 minutes, until pastry is well risen and golden brown.

Noisettes Provençales

PREPARATION TIME: 40 minutes

COOKING TIME: 35 minutes

8 noisettes of lamb
50g (2oz) butter
15ml (1 tblsp) oil

Provençale Sauce
50g (2oz) butter
15ml (1 tblsp) oil
1 large onion, finely chopped
1 clove garlic, crushed
450g (1lb) tomatoes, skinned and chopped
15ml (1 tblsp) tomato purée
150ml (¼ pint) dry white wine
Seasoning

Sauté the noisettes in the butter and oil for about 15 minutes, turning occasionally to brown the lamb on both sides.

This page: Stuffed Lamb Chops (top right), Lamb Chops and Mint Sauce (centre left) and Lamb and Kidney Pie (bottom).

Facing page: Moussaka (top), Rolled and Stuffed Breast of Lamb (centre) and Noisettes Provençales (bottom).

Provençale Sauce

Meanwhile, heat the butter with the oil and add the onion and garlic. Fry gently until soft but not brown. Stir in tomatoes, tomato purée and white wine and bring to the boil, stirring. Allow to cook uncovered over a fairly brisk heat for 10-15 minutes, stirring occasionally. Season to taste. Serve the sauce with the noisettes.

Risotto

PREPARATION TIME: 35 minutes	
COOKING TIME: 1 hour	

25g (1oz) butter
30ml (2 tblsp) oil
1 large onion, finely chopped
1 clove garlic, crushed
225g (8oz) long grain rice
100g (4oz) button mushrooms, sliced
200g (7oz) tin sweet corn and peppers
100g (4oz) frozen peas
1 whole green or red pepper, seeded, cored and chopped
350g (12oz) cooked lamb (leg or shoulder)
600ml (1 pint) chicken stock

Melt the butter with the oil. Add the onion and garlic and fry gently for 10-15 minutes until soft and golden brown. Stir in the rice and cook for a further 3-4 minutes, stirring continuously. Add the mushrooms, sweet corn and peppers, peas and the chopped red or green peppers. Cut the lamb into small pieces, add to the saucepan and mix well. Add the stock and bring to the boil. Reduce heat, cover and simmer for 35-40 minutes until the rice is cooked and the stock has been absorbed.

Winter Lamb

PREPARATION TIME: 35 minutes	
COOKING TIME: 1 hour 55 minutes	

1kg (2lb) scrag or best end of neck of lamb
50g (2oz) flour
50g (2oz) fat
2-3 onions, cut into rings
750ml (1¼ pint) brown stock
4-6 carrots, peeled and sliced
Seasoning
2.5ml (½ tsp) chopped mint
4 firm tomatoes, quartered
50-100g (2-4oz) mushrooms, sliced
Chopped parsley

Coat the lamb in the seasoned flour and fry for 2-3 minutes, add onions and continue cooking for a further 3 minutes. Stir in the stock gradually, bring to the boil and cook until thickened. Add carrots, seasoning and mint. Put lid on pan and simmer gently for 1½ hours. Add tomatoes and mushrooms and cook for 15 minutes. Garnish with chopped parsley.

Crown Roast of Lamb

PREPARATION TIME: 20 minutes	
COOKING TIME: 25 minutes per 450g (1lb) plus 25 minutes	

2 best ends of neck of lamb, chined
Stuffing (optional)
225g (8oz) button mushrooms
50g (2oz) butter
Cutlet frills

Trim the fat and skin from the ends of the rib bones, so that 2.5cm (1 inch) of bone protrudes. Place the joints back-to-back and sew the ends together, using fine string and a trussing needle, with the cutlet bones curving up and outwards. Most butchers will make the crown for you if given notice. If a stuffed joint is preferred, use your favourite stuffing to fill the crown roast. Cover the top of the crown of lamb with foil to keep the stuffing moist and to prevent the bones from burning during cooking. Roast at 180°C, 350°F, Gas Mark 4. Fry mushrooms in butter for 5-6 minutes. Remove the foil and top the stuffing with the mushrooms. Place a cutlet frill on each bone and serve.

Scandinavian Lamb

PREPARATION TIME: 50 minutes	
COOKING TIME: 1 hour 20 minutes	

1 breast of lamb, boned and cubed
15ml (1 tblsp) oil
1 medium onion, sliced
300ml (½ pint) stock
5ml (1 tsp) rosemary
Seasoning
15ml (1 tblsp) cornflour
150g (5oz) carton sour cream
150g (5oz) cooked peas

Fry the lamb in oil for 15-20 minutes. Remove from the pan and drain off most of the fat. Fry the onion in the remaining fat until soft. Return the lamb to the pan and add the stock, seasoning and rosemary. Bring to the boil, cover and simmer for 1 hour. Remove from the heat and add the sour cream and peas. This dish goes well with boiled rice.

Savoury Pudding

PREPARATION TIME: 40 minutes	
COOKING TIME: 2 hours 15 minutes	

1 onion, finely chopped
15ml (1 tblsp) oil
225g (8oz) minced lamb
15ml (1 tblsp) tomato purée
2.5ml (½ tsp) thyme
Seasoning
450ml (¾ pint) stock
1 large carrot, grated
350g (12oz) suet pastry
25g (1oz) cornflour
Gravy browning

Fry the onion and minced lamb in oil for 5 minutes, until mince is brown. Stir in the tomato purée, thyme, seasoning and stock and simmer for 10 minutes. Drain, reserving the stock. Add the carrot to the lamb mixture. Divide the pastry into three, and place one layer in the bottom of a greased 1,200ml (2 pint) basin. Place half the lamb mixture on top and repeat, finishing with a layer of suet pastry. Cover with buttered greaseproof paper or foil and steam for 2 hours. Mix cornflour with 30ml (2 tblsp) of cold water and add to reserved stock with a few drops of gravy browning. Bring to the boil, stirring continuously, and serve with the pudding.

Lamb Chops in Wine Sauce

PREPARATION TIME: 40 minutes	
COOKING TIME: 45 minutes	

25g (1oz) margarine or butter
4 loin chops
1 onion, sliced
5-10ml (1-2 tsp) paprika
150ml (¼ pint) dry white wine
150ml (¼ pint) chicken stock
15ml (1 tblsp) medium sherry
Seasoning
5ml (1 tsp) cornflour
50g (2oz) button mushrooms, sliced
2 tomatoes, skinned
Chopped parsley

Heat fat and brown chops on both sides. Drain and leave on one side. Add onion to pan and cook, with the paprika, until soft. Allow to cool slightly then pour on wine, stock and sherry. Return chops to pan, season well, bring to the boil, reduce heat and simmer, covered, for about 30 minutes. Blend cornflour with a little cold water and stir into wine and stock, stirring all the time. Add the mushrooms and tomatoes. Adjust seasoning and simmer for a further 15 minutes. Place chops on a serving dish, spoon over sauce and garnish with chopped parsley.

Crown Roast of Lamb (right),
Festive Leg of Lamb (below)
and Risotto (bottom).

Lamb Chops Reform

PREPARATION TIME: 35 minutes

COOKING TIME: 1 hour
10 minutes

8 lamb chops
25g (1oz) flour, seasoned
Beaten egg and breadcrumbs for
coating
Oil for deep frying

Reform Sauce
50g (2oz) butter
50g (2oz) streaky bacon, chopped
1 small onion, chopped
1 large tomato, quartered
1 small carrot, sliced
50g (2oz) plain flour
600ml (1 pint) brown stock
10ml (2 tsp) mushroom ketchup
(optional)
1 bouquet garni
Seasoning
15ml (1 tblsp) redcurrant jelly
15ml (1 tblsp) port

Trim and wipe chops. Dip them in seasoned flour and coat with egg and breadcrumbs.

Reform Sauce
Melt the butter in a saucepan. Add bacon and fry for 10 minutes. Add sliced vegetables until golden brown, stirring occasionally. Add flour and continue to fry slowly until a rich, brown colour. Add stock, mushroom ketchup and bouquet garni and simmer, covered, for 40 minutes. Skim and sieve the sauce. Add the redcurrant jelly and heat gently until the jelly dissolves. Stir in the port and check seasoning.

To Fry the Crumbed Cutlets
Heat a pan of cooking oil until hot. Place chops in the hot oil and fry for 1 minute. Turn off heat and allow the chops to continue cooking in the oil for a further 5 minutes. Drain well and arrange on a serving dish. Serve with the reform sauce.

Lamb Provençale

PREPARATION TIME: 30 minutes

COOKING TIME: 1 hour

450g (1lb) lamb from a cooked leg
50g (2oz) butter
15ml (1 tblsp) oil
2 medium onions, chopped
1 clove garlic, crushed
400g (14oz) tin tomatoes
15ml (1 tblsp) tomato purée

300ml (½ pint) dry white wine
100g (4oz) mushrooms, sliced
1 large green pepper, seeded and
sliced
Seasoning

Cut lamb into small cubes. Melt the butter with the oil and add onions and garlic. Fry gently for about 10-15 minutes until soft, but not brown. Stir in the tomatoes, tomato purée and wine. Bring to the boil and add the lamb. Simmer, covered, for 25 minutes. Add the mushrooms and green peppers and

cook for a further 15 minutes, stirring occasionally.

This page: Spare Ribs and Sweet and Sour Sauce (top), Lamb à l'Orange (centre left), Lamb Provençale (centre right) and Lamb Chops Reform (bottom). Facing page: Winter Lamb (top left), Scandinavian Lamb (top right), Irish Stew with Parsley Dumplings (centre left) and Lamb Chops in Wine Sauce (bottom right).

Lamb à l'Orange

PREPARATION TIME: 20 minutes

COOKING TIME: 25 minutes

1 small onion, finely chopped
15ml (1 tblsp) oil
l large orange
15ml (1 tblsp) redcurrant jelly
300ml (½ pint) stock
2.5ml (½ tsp) dry mustard
2.5ml (½ tsp) caster sugar
Pinch cayenne pepper
15ml (1 tblsp) cornflour

10ml (2 tsp) chopped parsley
30ml (2 tblsp) cold water

Coat the chops with seasoned flour and put them into a saucepan. Add the onion flakes and pearl barley. Sprinkle on the casserole seasoning and tuck in the bayleaf. Pour over the water and bring to the boil. Skim off any scum that rises to the surface. Reduce the heat, cover, simmer gently for 1 hour, add the potatoes and cook for a further 1½ hours.

Dumplings
Sift flour and seasoning into a bowl. Stir in suet and parsley, then add enough water to bind to a dough. Divide the dough into 4 large portions and shape into balls. About 20 minutes before the lamb has finished cooking, check that the liquid is boiling and drop dumplings into the pan. Replace the lid and finish the cooking at boiling point. Discard the bayleaf, adjust the seasoning and serve.

Spare Ribs and Sweet and Sour Sauce

PREPARATION TIME: 30 minutes

COOKING TIME: 50 minutes

4-8 spare ribs

Sauce
15g (½oz) cornflour
150ml (¼ pint) water
30ml (2 tblsp) vinegar from mixed pickles
Seasoning
15ml (1 tblsp) Worcestershire sauce
10ml (2 tsp) brown sugar

Garnish
Cooked rice
Lemon wedges

Put meat into roasting tim. Cook at 200°C, 400°F, Gas Mark 6, for about 30 minutes. Pour off surplus fat and return to oven for a further 15-20 minutes, until chops are crisp and brown.

Sauce
Blend cornflour with water, place all sauce ingredients in a pan and cook until thickened.

Garnish
Make a wide border of rice on a warm dish and arrange the spare ribs on this. Pour sauce into centre and place lemon wedges round the edge.

350g (12oz) cooked lamb, leg or shoulder

Fry onion gently in oil until soft, but not brown. Grate the orange rind. Cut three fine slices from the orange, trim the pith and reserve for garnish. Squeeze the juice from the remainder of the orange and add to the onion with the orange rind, redcurrant jelly and stock. Bring to the boil, reduce heat and cook, stirring, for 5 minutes. Blend the mustard, sugar, pepper and cornflour together with 30ml (2 tblsp) cold water and stir into the orange sauce. Slice the lamb, add to sauce and bring to the boil. Reduce heat and simmer for 15 minutes. When cooked, garnish with the reserved orange slices.

Irish Stew with Parsley Dumplings

PREPARATION TIME: 45 minutes

COOKING TIME: 2 hours 50 minutes

Irish Stew
1.3kg (3lb) middle neck lamb chops
15g (½oz) seasoned flour
30ml (2 tblsp) dried onion flakes
15ml (1 tblsp) pearl barley
10ml (2 tsp) casserole seasoning
1 bayleaf
600ml (1 pint) boiling water
225g (8oz) potatoes, cut into chunks

Dumplings
100g (4oz) self-raising flour
2.5ml (½ tsp) salt
1.25ml (¼ tsp) ground black pepper
50g (2oz) suet, finely shredded

Pork

Piquant Pork Chops

PREPARATION TIME: 30 minutes

COOKING TIME: 1 hour 10 minutes

4 pork chops
15ml (1 tblsp) oil
1 small onion, peeled and chopped
15ml (1 tblsp) brown sugar
15ml (1 tblsp) dry mustard
10ml (1 dsp) tomato purée
1 beef stock cube
300ml (½ pint) water
15ml (1 tblsp) Worcestershire sauce
30ml (2 tblsp) lemon juice

Put the chops in a baking tin or a wide, shallow casserole and bake uncovered at 190°C, 375°F, Gas Mark 4, for about 20 minutes. Meanwhile, heat the oil, add the onion and fry until browned. Add the sugar, mustard, tomato purée and crumbled beef stock cube. Mix well, then add water and stir till boiling. Add the Worcestershire sauce and lemon juice and check seasoning. Pour off any excess fat from the chops and pour the sauce over them. Cover and continue cooking in the oven at 180°C, 350°F, Gas Mark 3, for about 40-45 minutes.

Pork Steaks and Apple Sauce

PREPARATION TIME: 20 minutes

COOKING TIME: 25 minutes

4 pork steaks
Seasoning

Apple Sauce
450g (1lb) apples
150ml (¼ pint) water
15ml (1 tblsp) sugar
15g (½oz) butter or margarine

Season the pork steaks and fry or grill until cooked, turning often to ensure that they are cooked all the way through. Peel, core and thinly slice the apples. Put into a pan with the water, sugar and butter or margarine. Cook gently until soft, then rub through a sieve. Serve the apple sauce with the cooked pork steaks.

Piquant Pork Chops (top left), Pork Steaks and Apple Sauce (top right) and Pork Chops and Apple Chips (bottom).

Roast Leg of Pork

PREPARATION TIME: 20 minutes

COOKING TIME: 30 minutes per 450g (1lb) plus 30 minutes

1.25kg (2½lb) leg of pork
25g (1oz) dripping or cooking fat

Place meat in a roasting tin, season, and spread with dripping or cooking fat. Place in the centre of a preheated oven, 180°C, 350°F, Gas Mark 4. If a covered roasting tin is used, basting is not necessary, but if the joint is uncovered the meat should be basted every 20-30 minutes. The meat should be turned over, using two metal spoons, halfway through the cooking. When the meat is cooked, transfer to a large carving dish and keep hot.

Roast Half Leg of Pork

PREPARATION TIME: 15 minutes

COOKING TIME: 30 minutes per 450g (1lb) plus 30 minutes

Place meat in a roasting tin, season, and spread with dripping or cooking fat. Place in the centre of a preheated oven, 180°C, 350°F, Gas Mark 4. If a covered tin is used, basting is not necessary, but if the joint is uncovered the meat should be basted every 20-30 minutes. The meat should be turned over, using two metal spoons, halfway through the cooking. When the meat is cooked, transfer to a large carving dish and keep hot.

Savoury Bacon

PREPARATION TIME: 30 minutes

COOKING TIME: 45 minutes

250g (8oz) diced bacon (gammon or back)
3 spring onions, chopped
3 eggs
300ml (½ pint) milk
2.5ml (½ tsp) powdered sage
Seasoning
675g (1½lb) creamed potatoes
75g (3oz) cheese, grated

Fry onion until crisp. Beat eggs and add milk, sage, onion and seasoning. Grease an ovenproof dish and pipe creamed potatoes round the edge. Put the bacon in the centre of dish and pour the egg mixture over the bacon. Sprinkle the top with cheese. Bake in the centre of the oven at 190°C, 375°F, Gas Mark 5, for about 30 minutes until set, and the potato border has browned.

Spicy Pork Meatballs

PREPARATION TIME: 50 minutes
COOKING TIME: 40 minutes

675g (1½lb) minced pork
1 large onion, grated
Pinch garlic granules
50g (2oz) ground almonds
50g (2oz) fresh breadcrumbs
1 small egg, beaten
5ml (1 tsp) chopped parsley
1.25ml (¼ tsp) ground cinnamon
2.5ml (½ tsp) salt
2.5ml (½ tsp) black pepper
30ml (2 tblsp) medium sherry
15g (½oz) butter
60ml (4 tblsp) oil

Sauce
1 small onion, finely chopped
Pinch garlic granules
7.5ml (1½ tsp) soft brown sugar
4 tomatoes, skinned and chopped
½ green pepper, cored, seeded and sliced
½ red pepper, cored, seeded and sliced
1.25ml (¼ tsp) crushed chillis
1.25ml (¼ tsp) cayenne pepper
5ml (1 tsp) paprika
5ml (1 tsp) chopped parsley
300ml (½ pint) beef stock
10ml (2 tsp) cornflour
60ml (4 tblsp) medium sherry

Meatballs
Mix together the pork, onion, garlic granules, almonds, breadcrumbs, egg, parsley, cinnamon, seasoning and sherry. Combine well, then shape into about 40 walnut-sized balls. Melt the butter with half the oil in a frying pan. Add the meatballs in batches and fry gently until browned on all sides, taking care not to break up the meatball shapes. Remove from the pan with a slotted spoon and drain on paper towels.

Sauce
Heat the remaining oil in a saucepan, add the onion, garlic granules and brown sugar to the pan and fry until the onion is soft. Stir in the tomatoes, green and red peppers, crushed chillis, cayenne pepper, paprika and parsley and cook for a further 3 minutes. Add stock and bring to the boil, stirring occasionally. Dissolve the cornflour in the sherry and add to the pan. Simmer, stirring, until thickened. Add the meatballs to the sauce and shake the pan to coat well. Cover the pan and cook gently for 20-25 minutes or until the meatballs are cooked through. Taste and adjust seasoning before serving.

Pork Chops and Apple Chips

PREPARATION TIME: 40 minutes
COOKING TIME: 30 minutes

4 pork chops
Fat for deep frying
2 large cooking apples
A little flour

Grill or fry the chops for 15-20 minutes, turning frequently. Peel and core the apples and cut them into chips. Roll the chips in flour and fry in deep fat until cooked. Serve with the chops, at once.

Minced Pork Loaf

PREPARATION TIME: 45 minutes
COOKING TIME: 1 hour
                45 minutes

225g (½lb) aubergine
675g (1½lb) minced pork
1 onion, chopped
50g (2oz) fresh breadcrumbs
15ml (1 tblsp) chopped parsley
Seasoning
Pinch curry powder
Pinch garlic salt
1 egg, beaten

Preheat oven to 200°C, 400°F, Gas Mark 6. Bake the aubergine in its skin for 15 minutes. Cut in two and scoop out the pulp. Mix in a bowl with the meat, onion, breadcrumbs, parsley, seasoning, curry powder and garlic salt. Blend in the beaten egg. Place the meat mixture in a greased, oblong bread tin. Stand the tin on a baking tray half filled with water and bake for 1½ hours. Cool and turn out on to a dish.

Bacon and Onion Roll

PREPARATION TIME: 30 minutes
COOKING TIME: 2 hours
                15 minutes

1 large onion, chopped
5ml (1 tsp) powdered sage
Seasoning
1 rounded teacup fresh white breadcrumbs
25g (1oz) margarine, melted
4 bacon rashers, trimmed

Spicy Pork Meatballs (above right), Bacon and Onion Roll (right) and Minced Pork Loaf (top right).

Suet Pastry

225g (8oz) self-raising flour
5ml (1 tsp) baking powder
2.5ml (½ tsp) salt
Pinch of pepper
100g (4oz) finely shredded suet
150ml (¼ pint) water

Mix together the onion, seasonings and breadcrumbs. Stir in the margarine. For the pastry: sift the flour, baking powder and seasonings into a mixing basin. Add suet and stir in enough water to mix to a firm dough. Turn out on to a floured board and roll out to an oblong. Arrange bacon rashers over surface and spread with stuffing to within 2.5cm (1 inch) of edges. Moisten pastry edges and roll into a roly-poly about 20cm (8 inches) long. Pinch edges to seal. Wrap in greased, double-thickness greaseproof paper, folding into a large pleat the length of the roll to allow for expansion. Wrap loosely in kitchen foil. Steam briskly for 2 hours.

Curried Pork

PREPARATION TIME: 25 minutes

COOKING TIME: 40 minutes

175g (6oz) pasta (macaroni or shaped pasta)
Salt
450g (1lb) frozen mixed vegetables
450g (1lb) pork fillet, diced
30ml (2 tblsp) oil
1 large onion, chopped
1 green pepper
15ml (1 tblsp) black treacle
5-10ml (1-2 tsp) curry powder
Seasoning
Butter
1 onion, sliced into rings

Cook the pasta in 1½ litres (3 pints) of boiling, salted water until tender; strain and keep half on one side for a garnish. Cook the frozen vegetables in a little salted water until they begin to soften; strain. Toss the pork in the hot oil for 5 minutes, add the onion, green pepper, treacle, curry powder and seasoning, then lower heat and continue to cook for a further 5 minutes. Stir in the vegetables and half the pasta. Heat gently for 10 minutes. Serve in a border of pasta tossed in a little butter and garnish with sliced, raw onion rings.

Pork Croquettes

PREPARATION TIME: 30 minutes

COOKING TIME: 15 minutes

350g (12oz) cooked pork, minced
25g (1oz) butter or margarine
25g (1oz) flour
150ml (¼ pint) milk
10ml (2 tsp) chopped parsley
10ml (2 tsp) chopped gherkins
75g (3oz) soft, fresh breadcrumbs
Seasoning
Oil or fat to fry

To Coat
1 egg, beaten
50g (2oz) crisp breadcrumbs

Make a thick sauce of the butter or margarine, flour and milk, and add the parsley, gherkins and meat. Blend well, then stir in the breadcrumbs and seasoning. Allow the mixture to cool, form into eight finger shapes, brush with egg and coat in breadcrumbs. Fry in hot fat or oil until crisp and brown. Drain well on kitchen paper. Serve hot.

Shepherd's Pie

PREPARATION TIME: 40 minutes

COOKING TIME: 30 minutes

225-350g (8-12oz) cooked minced pork
25g (1oz) dripping or fat
1 onion, finely chopped
2 tomatoes, skinned and chopped
Good pinch of mixed herbs
Seasoning
150-300ml (¼-½ pint) stock
450g (1lb) mashed potato
25g (1oz) butter or margarine

Heat the fat or dripping and fry the onion for 3 minutes. Add the tomatoes and the meat and heat together for 2-3 minutes. Stir in the herbs, seasoning and stock. Put into a pie dish and cover with the mashed potato, forking this neatly over, or piping it. Scatter pieces of butter on the potatoes to help the topping to brown. Bake in the centre of the oven at 190°C, 375°F, Gas Mark 5, until crisp and brown on top.

Pork Fillet with Apricots

PREPARATION TIME: 30 minutes

COOKING TIME: 40 minutes

450g (1lb) pork fillet, cut into bite-size pieces
30ml (2 tblsp) seasoned flour
50g (2oz) butter
400g (14oz) tin apricot halves, drained and juice retained
30ml (2 tblsp) Worcestershire sauce
30ml (2 tblsp) demerara sugar
10ml (2 tsp) vinegar
10ml (2 tsp) lemon juice
120ml (8 tblsp) water
225g (8oz) long grain rice

Toss the pork pieces in seasoned flour. Heat the butter and fry the pork until lightly browned. Chop all but three of the apricot halves. Mix 120ml (8 tblsp) apricot juice with the Worcestershire sauce, sugar, vinegar, lemon juice and water. Add any remaining flour to the pork and pour in the apricot sauce and chopped fruit. Bring to the boil, stirring. Reduce heat, cover and simmer for about 15 minutes. Spoon pork and sauce onto a serving dish. Cook the rice in boiling, salted water and arrange in a border around the meat. Garnish with remaining apricot halves.

Cranberry Ham

PREPARATION TIME: 25 minutes

COOKING TIME: 15 minutes

4 thick slices cooked ham
25g (1oz) fat
30ml (2 tblsp) cranberry jelly or sauce

Heat the ham for 2-3 minutes in the hot fat or brush with melted fat and heat under the grill. Spread with the sauce or jelly and leave under a hot grill until the sauce bubbles; serve at once.

Bacon Pancakes

PREPARATION TIME: 20 minutes

COOKING TIME: 30 minutes

8 bacon rashers, de-rinded

Batter
100g (4oz) flour, preferably plain
Pinch of salt
1 egg
300ml (½ pint) milk

Sieve the flour and salt into a large basin, big enough for beating in the liquid. Add the egg to the basin, then add about a quarter of the milk. Stir carefully with a wooden spoon until the flour is blended. Beat hard until smooth. Add the rest of the liquid. When the batter becomes thinner use a flat egg whisk to aerate the mixture. Cook pancakes in the usual way. Meanwhile, fry or grill the bacon rashers and cut into pieces. Sandwich the pancakes with really crisp bacon and serve hot.

This page: Stuffed Loin of Pork (top), Pork Fillet with Apricots (centre left) and Curried Pork (bottom). Facing page: Bacon Pancakes (top), Pork Croquettes (centre left), Shepherd's Pie (centre right) and Cranberry Ham (bottom).

Stuffed Loin of Pork

PREPARATION TIME: 40 minutes

COOKING TIME: 25 minutes per 450g (1lb) plus 25 minutes

1.5kg (3lb) loin of pork, boned

Stuffing
100g (4oz) soft breadcrumbs
50g (2oz) suet, finely shredded
30ml (2 tblsp) chopped parsley
15ml (1 tblsp) chopped chives or
*   spring onions*
Seasoning
1 egg
A little oil or fat

Score the fat on the meat with a knife. Blend the stuffing ingredients together and then spread the stuffing over the meat carefully and roll it up. Brush the scored fat with melted fat or oil and sprinkle lightly with salt. Weigh after stuffing meat. Cook in a roasting tin at 220°C, 425°F, Gas Mark 7. Remove the meat to a hot dish when cooked, pour off the surplus fat, leaving just 15ml (1 tblsp) in the roasting tin and make a gravy with this.

Fluffy Baked Eggs and Bacon

PREPARATION TIME: 15 minutes

COOKING TIME: 15 minutes

4 slices of bread
Butter
4 eggs
Seasoning
8 bacon rashers, de-rinded

Toast the bread and spread with butter. Separate the egg yolks and whites. Whisk the whites until very stiff, seasoning well. Make the egg white into a ring on each slice of toast, drop a yolk in the centre and bake until set in oven at 190°C, 375°F, Gas Mark 5. Serve with grilled bacon.

This page: Belly of Pork Casserole (top), Pork Chops and Frankfurters (centre right) and Bacon and Sausage Plait (bottom left). Facing page: Bacon Chops with Pears (top), Pork with Sweet and Sour Sauce (centre left), Bacon Casserole (centre right) and Fluffy Baked Eggs and Bacon (bottom).

Bacon Casserole

PREPARATION TIME: 30 minutes

COOKING TIME: 40 minutes per 450g (1lb) plus 5 minutes to thicken

175-250g (6-9oz) bacon or ham per
*   person*
Ground black pepper or peppercorns
450g (1lb) mixed vegetables

Soak the bacon in cold water. Put into the casserole and cover with cold water. Add pepper or peppercorns and cover. Allow

about 40 minutes per 450g (1lb) for a wide, thin joint; a little longer if a thick joint is used. Bake at 170°C, 325°F, Gas Mark 3. Add vegetables during cooking.

Belly of Pork Casserole

PREPARATION TIME: 40 minutes

COOKING TIME: 2 hours
                      15 minutes

1 large onion, sliced
1 large cooking apple, peeled and
*   sliced*

675g (1½lb) belly of pork
30ml (2 tblsp) tomato purée
1 chicken stock cube
450ml (¾ pint) boiling water
A pinch of freshly-ground black
*   pepper*
A pinch of sage

Put the onion and apple into a casserole and put the meat on top. Mix the tomato purée and stock cube together, add boiling water and stir till stock cube has dissolved. Pour over meat in casserole, add pepper and sage. Cover and bake at 170°C, 325°F, Gas Mark 2, for about 2 hours.

Pork Kebabs

PREPARATION TIME: 25 minutes
COOKING TIME: 20 minutes

450g (1lb) lean pork, cut into bite-size pieces

Brush kebabs with melted butter and cook under the grill, turning the skewers to make sure that the food is well cooked. The food can be slipped from the skewer easily onto serving plates.

This is a most attractive way of serving grilled foods. You can thread a mixture of foods – kidneys, bacon, sausages, diced pork, mushrooms, onions, tomato halves, etc. – onto metal skewers.

Bacon Chops with Pears

PREPARATION TIME: 25 minutes
COOKING TIME: 20 minutes

6 gammon chops
3 dessert pears
25g (1oz) melted butter
15g (½oz) flour
1 egg, beaten
100g (4oz) breadcrumbs
Oil for deep frying

Brush the bacon with melted butter and grill for 4-5 minutes on both sides. Peel and core the pears and cut in halves. Coat pear halves with flour, then with egg and breadcrumbs. Fry in deep oil for 10 minutes until golden brown. Serve bacon with a pear half on each slice.

Bacon and Sausage Plait

PREPARATION TIME: 50 minutes
COOKING TIME: 30-40 minutes

350g (¾lb) rough-puff pastry, frozen

Filling
250g (8oz) pork sausage meat
250g (8oz) cooked bacon, chopped
2 hard-boiled eggs, roughly chopped
5ml (1 tsp) sage
Seasoning

Glaze
1 egg, beaten
A little salt

Roll the pastry out to a 25cm (10 inch) square. Mix all the ingredients together and place down the centre of the pastry, leaving equal sides of unfilled pastry. Cut the sides obliquely in 1cm (½ inch) strips and brush with beaten egg. Lift alternate strips over the sausage mixture to form a roll resembling a plait. Brush with egg and sprinkle with salt. Bake at 200°C, 400°F, Gas Mark 6, for about 15 minutes. Lower heat to 180°C, 350°F, Gas Mark 4, for a further 15 minutes.

Ham in Cider and Raisin Sauce

PREPARATION TIME: 45 minutes
COOKING TIME: 30 minutes per 450g (1lb) plus 30 minutes

2kg (4lb) forehock, ham or bacon
1 carrot, sliced
1 onion, sliced
Bouquet garni
3 whole cloves
600ml (1 pint) cider
600ml (1 pint) water

Cider and Raisin Sauce
100g (4oz) seedless raisins
300ml (½ pint) stock (from cooking bacon)
25g (1oz) brown sugar
2-3 drops gravy browning
Juice of ½ lemon
10ml (2 tsp) cornflour
30ml (2 tblsp) water

Put the ham, vegetables, herbs and cloves in the pan and add cider and water. Bring to the boil and cover. Simmer slowly, allowing 20 minutes per 450g (1lb) plus 20 minutes for ham, or 30 minutes per 450g (1lb) plus 30 minutes for forehock.

Cider and Raisin Sauce
Put all the sauce ingredients, except cornflour and water, into a saucepan. Cover and simmer for 10 minutes. Blend the cornflour with 30ml (2 tblsp) water. Stir into the sauce, simmer for a further 3 minutes. Serve sauce separately.

Pork Chops and Frankfurters

PREPARATION TIME: 30 minutes
COOKING TIME: 20 minutes

4 small pork chops (loin or spare ribs)
Seasoning
50-75g (2-3oz) melted butter
4-8 frankfurters
1 green pepper, cored and sliced
2 small eating apples, cored and sliced
350g (12oz) can sauerkraut
Parsley

Season pork chops. If they are lean, brush with a little melted butter and grill until tender, turning over and lowering the heat when browned on either side. Simmer the frankfurters in boiling water for 5 minutes; drain. Fry the green pepper and apples in the rest of the butter, add the sauerkraut and heat thoroughly. Put the apple mixture on to a hot dish, top with the chops and frankfurters and garnish with parsley.

Boiled Bacon and Pease Pudding

PREPARATION TIME: overnight plus 30 minutes
COOKING TIME: 2 hours

175-250g (6-9oz) bacon per person
Pepper

Pease Pudding
225g (8oz) dried split yellow peas
1 onion
2 cloves
Seasoning
100g (4oz) butter

Wash and soak salted bacon overnight, or for several hours, in cold water. Put soaked bacon into a saucepan, cover with cold water. Bring to the boil, skim, removing any greyish film floating on top. Add pepper, but no salt. Put a lid on the pan and cook slowly, allowing 30 minutes per 450g (1lb) for thinner joints, 35 minutes per 450g (1lb) for thicker joints.

Pease Pudding
Place split peas in a bowl, cover with cold water and soak for 3 hours. Rinse thoroughly. Peel the onion and press a clove into each end. Place the onion and split peas in boiling water. Do not salt. Simmer for ¾-1 hour or until peas are soft. Drain. Remove the cloves from the onion. Mash the peas and the onion together or pass them through a blender to form a smooth purée. Season well and beat in the butter.

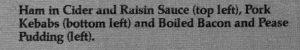

Ham in Cider and Raisin Sauce (top left), Pork Kebabs (bottom left) and Boiled Bacon and Pease Pudding (left).

Ham and Egg Pie

PREPARATION TIME: 50 minutes

COOKING TIME: 20-30 minutes

225g (8oz) shortcrust pastry
225g (8oz) lean cooked ham, finely
  chopped
6 eggs, lightly beaten
Seasoning
A little onion juice or minced onion
Beaten egg or milk to glaze

Line a pie plate with half the pastry. Mix the ham and eggs together, season and add the onion juice. Pour into the pastry case, damp the edges and cover with the remaining pastry, pressing edges well together. Brush with a little egg or milk and bake at 190°C, 375°F, Gas Mark 5, for 20 minutes, until pastry is golden brown.

Pork Pie

PREPARATION TIME: 50 minutes

COOKING TIME: 2 hours
                                    30 minutes

Hot Water Crust Pastry
350g (12oz) flour
Pinch of salt
140g (5oz) lard
150ml (¼ pint) water

Filling
100g (4oz) streaky bacon, diced
750g (1½lb) pork fillet, diced
Seasoning
Pinch of powdered ginger
15ml (1 tblsp) water

Jelly
600ml (1 pint) water
1 pig's trotter
1 bayleaf
1 onion

Pastry
Sieve the flour and salt into a mixing bowl. Heat the lard and water, cool slightly, then pour over the flour and knead well until smooth. Roll out two-thirds of the pastry for lining a cake tin (with loose base) or a raised pie tin that unlocks. Line the tin. Keep the rest of the pastry warm.

Filling
Fill with the bacon, pork, seasoning, ginger and water. Roll out the rest of the pastry and make a lid. Seal the edges firmly and make a centre slit. Brush the top

with beaten egg to give a glaze. Bake for about 2 hours until golden brown and firm, in the centre of the oven, 180°C, 350°F, Gas Mark 4.

Jelly
Boil the pig's trotter in the water with the onion and bayleaf until tender, then remove the onion and bayleaf and boil rapidly to give about 75ml (5 tblsp) strong liquid. Remove the pie from the tin, cool, allow stock to cool, then pour through centre hole with a funnel. Leave to set for 1 hour in refrigerator.

Apricot Glazed Gammon

PREPARATION TIME: 1 hour

COOKING TIME: 2 hours

2kg (4lb) gammon
2 bayleaves
Medium tin apricot halves
Watercress

Soak gammon for a few hours in cold water. Then place in an ovenproof dish with the bayleaves. Pour over enough boiling water to half cover the gammon. Cover the dish with foil and bake for 1¼

hours in the centre of the oven at 180°C, 350°F, Gas Mark 4. Remove from the oven and strain off the bacon stock. Remove the skin from the gammon and put the joint back into the ovenproof dish. Drain the juice from the apricots and pour it over gammon. Return the joint to the oven for another 45 minutes, basting frequently with the syrup. Remove the gammon from the oven and score diagonal designs on the fat with a sharp knife. Garnish with apricot halves and watercress.

Pork with Savoury Rice

PREPARATION TIME: 35 minutes

COOKING TIME: 40 minutes

4 good-sized pork chops
1 large onion, thinly sliced
50g (2oz) cooked long grain rice
3 large tomatoes, thickly sliced
Seasoning
300ml (½ pint) tinned or bottled
  tomato juice

Put the pork chops in an ovenproof dish and cook for 15 minutes at 190°C, 375°F, Gas Mark 5. Remove the dish from the oven and top with onion slices, then the rice, then the tomatoes. Season each layer well. Pour the tomato

juice into the dish. Return to the oven for a further 20-25 minutes, lowering the heat slightly if the mixture on top of the chops is becoming too brown.

Spare Ribs with Barbecue Sauce

PREPARATION TIME: 25 minutes

COOKING TIME: 45 minutes

8 pork spare ribs
25g (1oz) melted butter
Seasoning

Barbecue Sauce
25g (1oz) butter
2 onions, sliced
1 clove garlic, crushed
100g (4oz) mushrooms, chopped
Medium tin tomatoes
5ml (1 tsp) Worcestershire sauce
5ml (1 tsp) made mustard
2.5ml (½ tsp) mixed herbs
2.5ml (½ tsp) caster sugar
Seasoning

Garnish
Parsley

Brush chops with melted butter, season well. Grill for 15-20 minutes, turning once or twice and lowering heat after 10 minutes.

Barbecue Sauce
Melt butter in pan. Gently fry onions and garlic, add mushrooms and fry for a few minutes. Add tomatoes, Worcestershire sauce, mustard, herbs, sugar and seasoning. Simmer for about 10 minutes.

Garnish
Arrange chops on serving dish. Pour sauce over chops and garnish with fresh parsley.

Pork Steaks with Sweet and Sour Sauce

PREPARATION TIME: 25 minutes

COOKING TIME: 1 hour
                                    10 minutes

4 pork steaks

Sweet and Sour Sauce
15g (½oz) cornflour
150ml (¼ pint) water
30ml (2 tblsp) wine vinegar
Seasoning

Bacon and Corn Quiche

PREPARATION TIME: 40 minutes
COOKING TIME: 50 minutes

Shortcrust Pastry
175g (6oz) plain flour
Pinch of salt
75g (3oz) mixed margarine and lard
15-30ml (1-2 tblsp) cold water

Filling
15g (½oz) margarine
6 streaky bacon rashers, de-rinded
*   and chopped*
1 small onion, finely chopped
200g (7oz) tin sweet corn, drained
2 eggs
200ml (⅓ pint) milk
5ml (1 tsp) dried thyme
Seasoning

Pastry
Sift flour and salt into a mixing bowl. Cut in the lard and margarine and rub in until the mixture resembles breadcrumbs. Bind together with water to form a dough. Leave to rest for about 10 minutes. Roll out the dough to line a 23cm (9 inch) loose-bottom flan tin. Place a piece of greaseproof paper over the pastry and fill with 'blind' baking beans. Bake in a preheated oven, 200°C, 400°F, Gas Mark 6, for 10 minutes. Remove paper and beans and bake for a further ten minutes. Allow to cool.

Filling
Melt the margarine in a frying pan and fry bacon and onion until soft. Drain and place in the cooked flan case. Cover with the sweet corn. Beat the eggs and add the milk, herbs and seasoning to taste. Pour over the bacon and corn mixture. Cook in a hot oven 200°C, 400°F, Gas Mark 6, for 10 minutes. Reduce heat to 180°C, 350°F, Gas Mark 4 and bake for another 25 minutes.

Facing page: Spare Ribs with Barbecue Sauce (top), Pork with Savoury Rice (centre) and Bacon and Corn Quiche (bottom).

This page: Apricot Glazed Gammon (top), Pork Pie (centre right) and Ham and Egg Pie (bottom).

15ml (1 tblsp) Worcestershire sauce
10ml (2 tsp) brown sugar

Put chops into a roasting tin and roast at 200°C, 400°F, Gas Mark 6, for about 30 minutes. Pour off surplus fat and return to oven for a further 15-20 minutes until chops are crisp and brown.
Sweet and Sour Sauce
Blend cornflour with water, then put all ingredients for the sauce into a pan and cook until thickened. Serve sauce with cooked chops.

Veal

Veal Casserole

PREPARATION TIME: 30 minutes

COOKING TIME: 50 minutes

675g (1½lb) veal shoulder, cubed
Seasoning
50ml (2oz) chicken stock
2 large carrots
2 sticks celery, chopped
15ml (1 tblsp) quick tapioca
15ml (1 tblsp) water
4 slices of bread
Margarine

Season the veal. Bring chicken stock to the boil, add the meat, carrots and celery, cover and let simmer for 45 minutes. Mix the tapioca with the water, stir into the meat and simmer until the sauce thickens. Transfer to a casserole. Spread the bread slices with margarine on both sides and place on top of the casserole. Put in a hot oven until bread is toasted.

Veal en Croûte

PREPARATION TIME: 30 minutes

COOKING TIME: 55 minutes

Shortcrust Pastry
200g (7oz) flour
Pinch of salt
90g (3½oz) fat
Water to mix

Filling
75g (3oz) mushrooms, finely chopped
50g (2oz) butter
Seasoning
450-675g (1-1½lb) veal (in one piece)

Pastry
Sieve flour and salt together, rub in fat, bind with water and roll out to a large oblong.

Filling
Blend mushrooms with the butter and seasoning and spread over the centre of the pastry, leaving the ends plain. Put the veal on top, season lightly and wrap pastry round this. Seal the edges with water. Cook on a greased baking sheet for 20-25 minutes, in the

centre of the oven at 220-230°C, 425-450°F, Gas Mark 7-8. Lower heat to 180-190°C, 350-375°F, Gas Mark 4-5, for a further 30 minutes.

Veal Chops with Cheese

PREPARATION TIME: 35 minutes

COOKING TIME: 30 minutes

8 thick veal chops
100g (4oz) butter
Seasoning
400g (14oz) Gruyère cheese, grated
2 eggs
60ml (4 tblsp) double cream
Grated nutmeg
100ml (4 fl oz) white wine

Melt the butter in a large sauté pan with an ovenproof handle. Add the veal chops and sear them on both sides over a high heat. Reduce heat, season the chops, cover pan and cook gently for about 20

minutes, turning the chops once. In a bowl mix the cheese, eggs and cream. Season and add the nutmeg. Drain off the cooking butter from the pan and reserve it. Put some of the cheese mixture on each chop. Add the wine to the pan and place it, uncovered, in the oven, 190°C, 375°F, Gas Mark 5, for 10 minutes to finish the cooking. Baste the chops with the reserved cooking butter once or twice.

Fricassée of Veal

PREPARATION TIME: 25 minutes

COOKING TIME: 1 hour
                          20 minutes

675g (1½lb) veal cutlets
1 onion, stuck with cloves
Seasoning
Bouquet garni
25g (1oz) butter
25g (1oz) flour

Garnish
Bacon rolls
Lemon slices

Cut meat into small pieces and put in a saucepan, together with the onion, seasoning and bouquet garni. Cover with water, bring to the boil and simmer until the meat is tender (about 1 hour). Melt the butter in a pan, add the flour and stir well. Do not brown. Remove the bouquet garni and the onion from the veal. Add the liquid to the flour and fat, then add this to the veal. Cook gently for a further 10 minutes. Garnish with bacon rolls and lemon slices.

Veal and Mushroom Pie

PREPARATION TIME: 50 minutes

COOKING TIME: 2 hours
                          50 minutes

450g (1lb) veal, cubed
Seasoned flour
Butter or oil for frying
1 small bayleaf
175g (6oz) mushrooms, peeled and sliced
300ml (½ pint) stock
175g (6oz) shortcrust pastry
1 egg, beaten

Dust veal in seasoned flour. Fry until lightly brown. Add bayleaf and stock and bring to simmering point. Cover and cook in oven at 180°C, 350°F, Gas Mark 4, until tender (about 2 hours). Leave to cool. Roll pastry out to fit a large ovenproof plate. Put meat and mushrooms onto the plate, adding seasoning to taste. Cover with pastry. Brush with beaten egg to glaze. Bake at 230°C, 450°F, Gas Mark 8, for about 30 minutes.

This page: Veal and Mushroom Pie (top), Fricassée of Veal (centre left) and Veal en Croûte (bottom).

Facing page: Ragoût (top), Veal Chops with Mushrooms (centre right) and Veal Chops with Cheese (bottom).

Rolled Breast of Veal

PREPARATION TIME: 30 minutes

COOKING TIME: 1 hour
20 minutes

1.5kg (3lb) breast of veal, boned and trimmed
100g (4oz) smoked ham streaked with fat, finely chopped
50g (2oz) lard
90ml (6 tblsp) finely chopped parsley
1 garlic clove, crushed
Seasoning
200ml (7 fl oz) dry white wine

Score the inside of the breast crossways, in lines 3mm (⅛ inch) deep. Mix the smoked ham, 25g (1oz) of the lard, 60ml (4 tblsp) of the parsley, the garlic and 5ml (1 tsp) seasoning to make a paste. Spread the paste over the cut surface of the veal. Beginning at one of the narrow sides, roll up the veal tightly; skewer or tie with string. Season the surface of the meat. In a heavy pan, slowly brown the veal on all sides in the rest of the lard. Add the wine, cover and simmer for 1 hour or until tender. Remove the veal to a carving board and allow to stand for 10 minutes before cutting into slices. Skim any excess fat off the pan juices. Taste the juices, adjust the seasoning to taste, then reheat, adding the remaining parsley, and use as a sauce for the veal.

Veal Chops with Mushrooms

PREPARATION TIME: 45 minutes

COOKING TIME: 1 hour
10 minutes

4 veal chops
Seasoning
30ml (2 tblsp) oil
4 medium-sized carrots, sliced
100g (4oz) mushrooms, sliced
1 small onion, sliced
60ml (4 tblsp) white wine
2 tomatoes, peeled and sliced

Trim chops and season. Heat oil, brown chops on both sides, then transfer to a casserole. Add all other ingredients and cook in the oven at 170°C, 325°F, Gas Mark 3, for about 1 hour.

Fried Veal with Rice

PREPARATION TIME: 30 minutes

COOKING TIME: 1 hour

4 neck cutlets
Seasoned flour
1 small onion
1 small green pepper
1 stick celery
1 tomato
75g (3oz) fat or oil
150ml (¼ pint) stock
225g (8oz) rice

Toss the cutlets in seasoned flour. Peel and chop the onion and chop other vegetables. Melt 50g (2oz) fat and fry the veal until brown on both sides. Add the stock; simmer the meat until it is tender (45 minutes). Boil the rice. Melt 25g (1oz) fat and fry the onion, green pepper and celery. Stir in the cooked rice and add the tomato. Serve the cutlets on top of the rice mixture and pour over the juices from the frying pan.

Veal Chops with Wine (above), Fried Veal with Rice (right) and Roast Best End of Neck (far right).

Roast Best End of Neck

PREPARATION TIME: 10 minutes

COOKING TIME: 25 minutes per 450g (1lb) plus 25 minutes

Place joint in a roasting tin and spread with dripping or cooking fat and season. Place in the centre of a preheated oven. If a covered roasting tin is used, basting is not necessary, but if the joint is uncovered, the meat should be basted every 20-30 minutes. The meat should be turned over, using two metal spoons, halfway through the cooking. When the meat is cooked, transfer to a large carving dish and keep hot.

Veal Chops with Wine

PREPARATION TIME: 30 minutes

COOKING TIME: 1 hour 20 minutes

4 veal chops
40g (1½oz) flour
Seasoning
30ml (2 tblsp) oil
1 onion, chopped
100g (4oz) mushrooms, sliced
300ml (½ pint) white wine

Trim chops and coat with seasoned flour. Heat oil, brown chops on both sides, then transfer to a casserole. Add onion to remaining oil and cook till lightly brown. Add remaining flour and mix well. Add mushrooms and wine and bring to boiling point, stirring all the time. Pour sauce over chops in the casserole. Cover and cook for about 1 hour at 180°C, 350°F, Gas Mark 3.

Blanquette of Veal with Prunes

PREPARATION TIME: 20 minutes

COOKING TIME: 30 minutes

450g (1lb) veal, diced
2 onions, diced
1 sachet of bouquet garni
600ml (1 pint) white stock
50g (2oz) butter
50g (2oz) flour
150ml (¼ pint) cream or evaporated milk
1-2 egg yolks
15ml (1 tblsp) lemon juice

Garnish
Freshly cooked prunes
Freshly cooked vegetables

Put the veal, onions and herbs into a pan with the stock. Simmer gently until tender. Strain; keep the meat hot. Make a sauce with the butter, flour and stock; cook for 2 minutes. Add the cream or evaporated milk and reheat. Stir in the egg yolks and lemon juice. Reheat, but do not boil. Pour over the veal. Garnish with the prunes and vegetables.

Veal Roll with Prune and Apple Stuffing

PREPARATION TIME: 40 minutes

COOKING TIME: 1 hour
                              15 minutes

350g (12oz) shortcrust pastry
450-675g (1-1½lb) veal fillet

Stuffing
100g (4oz) bacon, de-rinded and
  chopped
100g (4oz) soft breadcrumbs
5ml (1 tsp) mixed herbs
175g (6oz) soaked prunes, drained
  well
1 medium dessert apple
Seasoning
1 egg yolk

Glaze
1 egg white

Roll out pastry to an oblong about
20x15cm (8x6 inches). Flatten veal
with a rolling pin into an oblong
about 5mm (¼ inch) thick. Fry
bacon for about 5 minutes, then
mix with other stuffing ingredients.
Spread over veal, then roll. Lay
onto the pastry, brush sides with
water and roll. Seal edges firmly.
Brush with leftover egg white to
glaze. Cook on a baking sheet for
20-25 minutes at 220°C, 425°F,
Gas Mark 7, then lower the heat to
180-190°C, 350-375°F, Gas Mark
4-5, for 45 minutes.

Veal Escalopes

PREPARATION TIME: 30 minutes

COOKING TIME: 15 minutes

4 thin slices veal, approx. 350g
  (12oz) each
1 egg, beaten
75g (3oz) white breadcrumbs
75g (3oz) Cheddar cheese, finely
  grated
Pinch of salt
Dash cayenne pepper
50g (2oz) vegetable shortening
50g (2oz) butter

Trim the veal slices to give neat
shapes and dip them in the beaten
egg. Mix the breadcrumbs and
grated cheese together and season
with salt and cayenne pepper. Use
this to coat the veal. Fry the veal
on both sides in hot vegetable
shortening for about 10 minutes,
till golden brown.

Veal Rolls

PREPARATION TIME: 30 minutes

COOKING TIME: 2 hours
                              15 minutes

4 veal escalopes
25g (1oz) melted butter
Seasoning
10ml (2 tsp) onion, finely chopped
5ml (1 tsp) grated lemon rind
10ml (2 tsp) parsley, finely chopped

Sauce
25g (1oz) butter
1 small onion, grated or finely
  chopped
½ small apple, peeled and grated
10ml (2 tsp) cornflour
1 small tin tomato purée
1 chicken stock cube
450ml (¾ pint) water

Brush the escalopes with a little
butter and sprinkle with seasoning,
onion, parsley and lemon, and roll
up tightly. Secure with a small
skewer or thin string. Put into a
casserole. To make the sauce heat
the butter, add the onion and
apple, and sauté for a few minutes
without browning. Stir in the
cornflour, tomato purée and
crumbled chicken stock cube and

**This page: Ginger Veal Chops
(top), Rolled Breast of Veal
(centre left) and Veal Marengo
(bottom right).**

**Facing page: Blanquette of Veal
with Prunes (top right), Veal
Rolls (centre left), Veal
Casserole (centre right) and
Veal Escalopes (bottom).**

mix well together. Add the water
and stir till boiling. Boil for 2
minutes, then pour over veal rolls.
Cover and cook at 170°C, 325°F,
Gas Mark 2, for about 2 hours.

Veal Marengo

PREPARATION TIME: 30 minutes

COOKING TIME: 1 hour
                              20 minutes

450g (1lb) neck of veal
Seasoned flour
75g (3oz) butter
2 onions, chopped
300ml (½ pint) white stock
225g (8oz) tomatoes, skinned and
  chopped
50g (2oz) mushrooms, chopped
Seasoning

Garnish
4 slices of bread, cut into croûtons
Fat for frying
Parsley
Lemon

Cut the veal into cubes. Coat with
seasoned flour and fry until golden
brown in hot butter. Add the
onion and fry until transparent.
Add the stock, tomatoes and
mushrooms. Season well. Simmer
gently for about 1 hour. Serve
garnished with croûtons of fried
bread, parsley and lemon.

Ginger Veal Chops

PREPARATION TIME: 30 minutes

COOKING TIME: 30 minutes

4 veal chops
Meat tenderizer
30ml (2 tblsp) margarine
1 tin condensed cream of celery soup
1 small tin peas or mixed vegetables
4 slices mild cheese
2.5ml (½ tsp) ginger

Tenderize veal following package
directions. In a covered pan slowly
sauté veal in margarine, turning to
brown on both sides. When meat
is tender, add soup and vegetables
to pan. When thoroughly heated,
place a slice of cheese on each veal
chop and sprinkle top with ginger.
Place under grill, or cover pan and
cook, until cheese melts.

Ragoût

PREPARATION TIME: 30 minutes

COOKING TIME: 1 hour
                              5 minutes

450g (1lb) stewing veal and kidney,
  diced
50g (2oz) dripping
2 onions, sliced
50g (2oz) mushrooms or 2 sliced,
  seeded red or green peppers
1 large tin cream of tomato soup
15ml (1 tsp) paprika
½ teacup water
Seasoning
Chopped parsley

Heat the dripping in a pan and fry
the veal and kidney, onions and
peppers for a few minutes. Cover
with the tomato soup and the
paprika blended with water. Add
seasoning to taste, cover, and
simmer for about 1 hour. Garnish
with chopped parsley, if desired.

Offal

Calves' Brains

PREPARATION TIME: 10 minutes
COOKING TIME: 35 minutes

450g (1lb) calves' brains
15ml (1 tblsp) vinegar

White Sauce
25g (1oz) cornflour
600ml (1 pint) milk
45ml (3 tblsp) white wine

Soak brains in cold water for 1 hour. Remove skin and traces of blood. Place brains in fresh water, to which 15ml (1 tblsp) of vinegar has been added and boil for 15-20 minutes. Drain and put in cold water to cool. Dry and slice.

White Sauce
Put the cornflour into a basin. Blend it to a thin cream with some of the milk, using a wooden spoon.

Rinse a saucepan with cold water; this prevents milk from sticking to the pan. Heat the milk to boiling point and pour over the blended cornflour, stirring all the time; add the white wine. Rinse the pan, return the mixture to the pan and boil for 3-5 minutes. Serve the brains with the white sauce, adding chopped carrot and runner beans if desired.

Liver and Onions

PREPARATION TIME: 15 minutes
COOKING TIME: 20 minutes

675g (1½lb) onions
6 slices of lamb's liver
Seasoning
45ml (3 tblsp) plain flour
75g (3oz) butter
30ml (2 tblsp) chopped parsley
  (optional)

Peel and slice the onions. Trim and wipe the liver. Season the flour and use it to coat the liver. Melt the butter in a large frying pan. Add the onions and fry till golden. Add the liver slices and fry for 3-10 minutes on each side. Stir in the parsley, if desired. Transfer to a warmed serving dish and top with fried onions. Spoon pan juices over.

Haggis

PREPARATION TIME: 50 minutes
COOKING TIME: 2 hours
                    40 minutes

225g (8oz) sheep's liver
100g (4oz) beef suet
2 onions
1 breakfast cup oatmeal
Seasoning

Cover the liver with water and boil for 40 minutes. Drain and keep the liquid. Mince the liver finely. Parboil the onions, then chop them finely with the suet. Brown the oatmeal by tossing it quickly in a thick pan. Combine the minced liver, suet, onions and oatmeal and season. Moisten with the liquor in which the liver was boiled. Turn into a greased bowl, cover with greaseproof paper and steam for 2 hours.

Calves' Brains (far left), Kidney and Sausage Casserole (centre) and Haggis (above).

Liver and Bacon Kebabs

PREPARATION TIME: 20 minutes

COOKING TIME: 5-10 minutes

350g (12oz) piece of lamb's liver
175g (6oz) piece of streaky bacon
100g (4oz) button mushrooms
50g (2oz) melted butter
50g (2oz) fine breadcrumbs
2.5ml (½ tsp) paprika
Salt

Wipe and trim the liver. Cut it into 2.5cm (1 inch) cubes. De-rind the bacon, cut it into thick rashers, then into squares. Wipe and trim mushrooms. Preheat the grill. Line the grill pan with foil. Thread the bacon, liver and mushrooms onto four skewers. Brush with melted butter. Mix the breadcrumbs, paprika and salt together on a plate. Turn the kebabs in the breadcrumbs till evenly coated. Arrange on the grill pan and grill for about 5 minutes, turning the kebabs frequently and brushing them with the fat that runs from the bacon.

Piquant Kidneys

PREPARATION TIME: 10 minutes

COOKING TIME: 15 minutes

450g (1lb) calves' kidneys
1 onion, finely chopped
50g (2oz) butter
30ml (2 tblsp) chopped parsley
15ml (1 tblsp) wine vinegar
Seasoning

Prepare and wash the kidneys. Slice very thinly. Melt the butter in a frying pan and cook the onion and parsley for 5 minutes. Add the kidneys and cook for a further 5-10 minutes, stirring occasionally. Stir in the vinegar and bring to the boil, then remove from heat immediately. Add seasoning to taste.

This page: Chicken Liver Omelette (top), Lambs' Hearts with Walnut Stuffing (bottom right) and Piquant Kidneys (bottom left).

Facing page: Liver and Bacon Kebabs (top), Sweetbread Fritters (centre left) and Liver, Bacon and Onion (bottom right).

Tongue and Lentil Casserole

PREPARATION TIME: 4 hours 30 minutes

COOKING TIME: 2 hours 45 minutes

225g (8oz) lentils, soaked overnight
4 sheep's tongues
25g (1oz) fat
2 onions, chopped
225g (8oz) carrots, chopped
Pinch of mixed herbs
Seasoning
1 clove garlic, crushed

Soak the sheep's tongues for 3-4 hours. Drain, cover with cold water and bring to the boil. Simmer for 10-15 minutes. Drain, cover with fresh, cold water and simmer for 1 hour. Pour off and retain water. Leave tongues to cool, then remove skin. Slice tongues and put into a casserole. Melt the fat, add the onions and fry till brown, then add to the tongues. Add the drained lentils and carrots to the fat and fry for a few minutes. Put into the casserole with the herbs, seasoning and garlic. Cover with stock. Cover the casserole and cook in oven at 170°C, 325°F, Gas Mark 3, for 1½ hours.

Lambs' Hearts with Walnut Stuffing

PREPARATION TIME: 30 minutes

COOKING TIME: 1 hour 25 minutes

4 lambs' hearts
4 large onions
Stock
Butter or margarine

Walnut Stuffing
50g (2oz) fresh breadcrumbs
50g (2oz) chopped walnuts
50g (2oz) fat bacon
Seasoning
Pinch mace
Egg to bind
150ml (¼ pint) stock
25g (1oz) butter or margarine
4 large onions

Put all the stuffing ingredients into a small basin and add sufficient egg to bind. Prepare the hearts by cutting away all tough skin, etc. Stuff the hearts and tie the ends with thread. Simmer gently for 1 hour in a little well-seasoned stock, with the onions. Place in a fireproof dish, pour over the remainder of the stock, place a little butter or margarine on top of the hearts and onions, cover with a lid. Roast at 190°C, 375°F, Gas Mark 5, for about 20 minutes. Cut away thread before serving.

Braised Oxtail

PREPARATION TIME: 30 minutes

COOKING TIME: 2 hours 45 minutes

1 oxtail
25g (1oz) margarine
2 carrots
2 large onions
1 rasher bacon
300ml (½ pint) stock
Seasoning

Wash the oxtail in cold water. Cut into sections. Fry the oxtail in melted margarine until browned. Prepare and slice the vegetables and arrange them in layers, alternately with the meat, finishing with a layer of vegetables. Season each layer. Pour the stock into the dish and braise slowly for about 2-2½ hours at 170°C, 325°F, Gas Mark 3.

Pig's Trotters

PREPARATION TIME: 10 minutes

COOKING TIME: 30-45 minutes

Cook the trotters in water with a bouquet garni. Simmer until tender. Drain well. Brush with melted butter, season and grill until golden brown. Serve with mashed potatoes and vegetables.

Sweetbread Fritters

PREPARATION TIME: 30 minutes

COOKING TIME: 10 minutes

450g (1lb) prepared lamb's sweetbreads
Seasoning
60ml (4 tblsp) plain flour
Oil for deep frying

Batter
2 egg whites
30ml (2 tblsp) arrowroot
5ml (1 tsp) chopped fresh chives
5ml (1 tsp) chopped fresh tarragon

Cut the sweetbreads in half lengthways. Season the flour and toss the sweetbreads in it till evenly coated. Shake off any excess flour. Heat the oil in a deep fryer to 170°C, 340°F. Put the egg whites into a bowl and whisk till soft peaks form. Add the arrowroot and herbs and fold in gently with a metal spoon. Fold in the floured sweetbreads till coated with batter. Using two spoons, lift a few of the sweetbreads out of the batter and lower into the oil. Fry for 5-6 minutes till crisp and golden. Drain on kitchen paper, keep hot while you cook the rest, and serve.

Kidney and Sausage Casserole

PREPARATION TIME: 30 minutes

COOKING TIME: 2 hours 50 minutes

675g (1½lb) ox kidney
225g (8oz) pork sausages
25g (1oz) flour
Seasoning
50g (2oz) fat
1 medium onion, sliced
2 carrots, sliced
1 bayleaf
2.5ml (½ tsp) sage, crushed
300ml (½ pint) stock

Trim and core the kidneys. Cover with cold, salted water and leave for 15 minutes. Drain and dry. Cut the sausages into pieces. Season the flour and coat the kidneys and sausages well. Heat the fat and fry the meat till brown. Remove to a casserole. Add the onion and carrots to the fat and brown well, then place in the casserole. Add the bayleaf and sage. Put the remaining flour with the sediment left in pan, mix well, add the stock and stir till boiling. Pour over the meat in the casserole. Cover and cook at 170°C, 325°F, Gas Mark 2, for about 2½ hours. Adjust seasoning before serving.

Kidney and Sausage Casserole (top), Pig's Trotters (centre) and Tongue and Lentil Casserole (bottom).

Tripe and Onion Pie

PREPARATION TIME: 45 minutes

COOKING TIME: 1 hour

450g (1lb) tripe
3 large onions, chopped
300ml (½ pint) water
25g (1oz) flour
30ml (2 tblsp) milk
Seasoning
25g (1oz) butter
225g (8oz) shortcrust pastry

Place the chopped onion in a pan, cover with water, season and simmer until tender. Wash the tripe and cut it into small pieces. Strain the onions; reserve half of the liquid. Replace the onions and liquid in the pan. Add the tripe. Simmer for 15 minutes. Blend the flour with a little cold milk, add to the saucepan, stir continually; add remaining milk and butter. Cook for 5 minutes. Line a dish or tin with half the pastry, put in the filling, cover with the remaining pastry. Cook at 220°C, 425°F, Gas Mark 7, for 25 minutes.

Savoury Sheeps' Hearts

PREPARATION TIME: 40 minutes

COOKING TIME: 2 hours
                                    15 minutes

4 sheep's hearts
Stuffing
50g (2oz) butter
1 onion, chopped
1 stick celery, chopped
100g (4oz) breadcrumbs
1 orange
Seasoning
1 egg, beaten
2 onions, cut into quarters or eighths
2 carrots, cut into quarters
1 beef stock cube
600ml (1 pint) boiling water

Prepare the hearts carefully, removing all the veins and arteries, and wash them well in cold water. Melt the butter, add the onion and celery and cook for a few minutes. Add the breadcrumbs, grated orange rind and juice, and seasoning. Bind with the egg. Fill the hearts with this stuffing and sew up with needle and thread. Put into a casserole with the onion and carrot pieces. Dissolve the stock cube in boiling water and pour over the hearts. Cover and cook at 170°C, 325°F, Gas Mark 3, for 2 hours until tender. Remove thread before serving.

Chicken Liver Omelette

PREPARATION TIME: 20 minutes

COOKING TIME: 30 minutes

100g (4oz) chicken livers
100g (4oz) butter
2 sage leaves
Seasoning
45ml (3 tblsp) sherry
8 eggs
Parsley

Trim, wipe and finely chop the livers. Melt 25g (1oz) of the butter in a saucepan and add the livers. Stir fry for 5 minutes. Pour the sherry over and cook till it has almost evaporated. Remove pan from heat. Beat the eggs in a bowl with a little seasoning. Melt a quarter of the remaining butter in an omelette pan or small frying pan. When it begins to foam, pour in a quarter of the egg mixture. Tilt the pan so that the mixture runs evenly over the bottom. As the omelette begins to set underneath, place a quarter of the liver mixture along the centre and fold the sides of the mixture over the filling. Slide omelette onto a warmed serving dish and keep hot.

Braised Oxtail (top), Savoury Sheeps' Hearts (centre right) and Tripe and Onion Pie (bottom left).

Poultry and Game

Turkey Fries

PREPARATION TIME: 45 minutes

COOKING TIME: 1 hour
                              10 minutes

60ml (4 tblsp) oil
45ml (3 tblsp) lemon juice
Salt
8x125g (8x4oz) slices of turkey
    breast
20ml (4 tsp) Dijon mustard
2 eggs
225g (8oz) fresh breadcrumbs
50g (2oz) butter

Garnish
Chopped parsley
Lemon wedges

Mix half the oil with the lemon
juice and a pinch of salt in a
shallow dish. Add the turkey, mix
well and leave to marinate for 1
hour. Drain the turkey and pat dry
on kitchen paper. Spread thinly
with the mustard. Beat the eggs
lightly on a plate and use to coat
turkey. Dip the turkey slices into
the breadcrumbs, pressing on them
gently. Melt the butter and
remaining oil in a frying pan and
gently fry the turkey for about 10
minutes on each side, till tender
and golden brown. Drain. Garnish
with chopped parsley and lemon
wedges.

Roast Chicken Drumsticks

PREPARATION TIME: 10 minutes

COOKING TIME: 20-30 minutes

Place the chicken drumsticks in a
roasting tin and spread with fat or
oil. Season. Place in the oven at
180°C, 350°F, Gas Mark 4, for
about 20-30 minutes until the juice
runs clear and the skin is golden
brown.

**Turkey Roll (top) and Turkey
Fries (bottom).**

Roast Turkey

PREPARATION TIME: 10 minutes

COOKING TIME: 20 minutes per 450kg (1lb) plus 20 minutes

Place the turkey in a roasting tin. Brush with melted fat or oil. Season. Lightly cover the bird with foil or double greaseproof paper. The bird may be stuffed if desired but weigh it after stuffing to calculate cooking time. Place in the oven at 200°C, 400°F, Gas Mark 6, for the first 15 minutes, then lower to 180°C, 350°F, Gas Mark 4, for the remainder of the cooking time. Baste the turkey frequently. Remove covering for the last 20-30 minutes to allow the skin to brown. When the turkey is cooked, place it on a large carving dish and serve.

Chicken Casserole

PREPARATION TIME: 30 minutes

COOKING TIME: 2 hours
40 minutes

1 chicken, jointed
Seasoned flour
25g (1oz) dripping
1 carrot, sliced
1 turnip, sliced
1 onion, chopped
25g (1oz) flour
600ml (1 pint) stock
Bouquet garni
Seasoning

Toss the chicken joints in seasoned flour. Melt the dripping, brown the vegetables and the joints. Remove them from the pan. Add the flour but do not brown. Remove from heat and add stock. Return to heat and bring to the boil. Season to taste. Put vegetables and chicken in a casserole dish, pour sauce over, add the bouquet garni. Cook at 180°C, 325°F, Gas Mark 3, for about 2½ hours.

This page: Rabbit Casserole (top), Roast Guinea Fowl (bottom). Facing page: Roast Chicken Drumsticks (top right), Roast Turkey (centre) and Chicken Casserole (bottom right).

Chicken Pieces in Breadcrumbs

PREPARATION TIME: 30 minutes

COOKING TIME: 35-40 minutes

4 chicken quarters
Seasoning
50g (2oz) flour
1 egg
300ml (½ pint) milk
175g (6oz) breadcrumbs
45ml (3 tblsp) oil

Clean the chicken quarters and dredge with the seasoned flour. Beat the eggs in a bowl and mix in the milk. Dip the chicken pieces in the egg and milk and then coat with the breadcrumbs. Heat the oil in a frying pan and fry the chicken for 10 minutes or until browned on both sides. Reduce the heat, cover the pan and continue cooking gently for 25-30 minutes until the chicken is tender.

Roast Turkey Legs

PREPARATION TIME: 10 minutes

COOKING TIME: 30-40 minutes

Place the turkey legs in a roasting tin and spread with fat or oil. Season. Cook in the oven at 190°C, 375°F, Gas Mark 5, for about 30 minutes, until the juice runs clear and the skin is golden brown.

Roast Guinea Fowl

PREPARATION TIME: 10 minutes

COOKING TIME: 15 minutes per 450g (1lb)

Place the guinea fowl in a roasting tin and brush with melted fat or oil. Season. As guinea fowl can be very dry, be generous in the amount of fat used. Lightly cover the bird with foil or double greaseproof paper and cook at 200°C, 400°F, Gas Mark 6. Baste frequently. Remove the covering for the last 20-30 minutes to allow the skin to brown. When the bird is cooked, place it on a warm carving dish and serve.

Rabbit Casserole

PREPARATION TIME: 30 minutes

COOKING TIME: 2 hours 20 minutes

1.5kg (3lb) rabbit
25g (1oz) seasoned flour
50g (2oz) butter
100g (4oz) shallots, chopped
2 carrots, sliced
2 parsnips, sliced
1 small cooking apple, peeled, cored and chopped
600ml (1 pint) cider
15ml (1 tbsp) made mustard
10ml (2 tsp) casserole seasoning
2.5ml (½ tsp) thyme
Seasoning
1 bayleaf

Preheat the oven to 180°C, 350°F, Gas Mark 4. Cut the rabbit into six serving pieces. Coat with the seasoned flour. Melt the butter in a flameproof casserole. Add the rabbit and brown on all sides. Remove the rabbit from the pan, then add the shallots, carrots, parsnips and apple and fry until lightly coloured. Pour in the cider, stir in the mustard and casserole seasoning. Heat gently, stirring, until just simmering, then return the rabbit pieces to the pan. Add the thyme and the bayleaf, cover the casserole and place it in the oven. Cook for 1½-2 hours, until the rabbit is tender. Taste and adjust the seasoning and discard the bayleaf.

Roast Pheasant

PREPARATION TIME: 10 minutes

COOKING TIME: 40 minutes to 1 hour 30 minutes

Preheat the oven to 200°C, 400°F, Gas Mark 6. Stand prepared bird in a roasting tin, add a little dripping or oil. Cover roasting tin or wrap bird in foil. Roast a young bird for 40-50 minutes, an older bird for 1-1½ hours. Reduce the oven temperature to 180°C, 350°F, Gas Mark 4, after 10 minutes. If the bird is cooked in an open tin, baste frequently.

Game Pie

PREPARATION TIME: 40 minutes

COOKING TIME: 45 minutes

1 rabbit
4 bacon rashers, de-rinded
50g (2oz) dripping
2 onions, sliced
Seasoning
300ml (½ pint) stock
225g (8oz) flaky pastry
1 egg or milk to glaze

Soak the rabbit in warm water for about ½ hour. Wash well in cold water. Joint the rabbit into 6 pieces. Cut the bacon into large pieces. Melt the dripping in a saucepan. First brown the onions, then the bacon and pieces of rabbit. Season well. Add the stock and simmer gently for 1 hour until tender. Leave to cool. When cool, fill a pie dish with the meat and onions, add the liquid, then cover with the flaky pastry. Bake at 200°C, 400°F, Gas Mark 6, for ¾ hour. Brush with egg or milk during the last ½ hour.

Roast Turkey Legs (right), Chicken Pieces in Breadcrumbs (below).

Fricassée of Guinea Fowl

PREPARATION TIME: 30 minutes

COOKING TIME: 1 hour
30 minutes

1 guinea fowl
4 slices bacon
30ml (2 tbsp) flour
Seasoning
2 cups water

Clean the guinea fowl and joint into pieces. Fry the bacon, coat the pieces of fowl with seasoned flour and fry until brown. Remove the bacon and fowl from the pan, add the flour and stir, slowly adding the water. Bring to the boil. Replace the fowl and bacon, cover and simmer until tender (about 1½ hours).

Jugged Hare

PREPARATION TIME: 30 minutes

COOKING TIME: 3 hours
10 minutes

1 hare
1 onion, sliced
1 carrot, sliced
1 turnip, sliced
75g (3oz) fat
75g (3oz) flour
Seasoning
600ml (1 pint) stock
15ml (1 tbsp) port
Bouquet garni
Packet of sage and onion stuffing mix

Wash and joint hare. Fry the vegetables in fat. Remove vegetables from the pan, coat the hare in seasoned flour and fry. Add the stock and port, put into the casserole with the bouquet garni, cover and cook for about 3 hours at 180°C, 350°F, Gas Mark 4. Making stuffing as directed on packet and make into small balls. Add balls to casserole a quarter of an hour before serving.

Roast Stuffed Pigeons

PREPARATION TIME: 30 minutes

COOKING TIME: 35 minutes to 1
hour 15 minutes

4 small pigeons
40-50g (1½-2oz) lard

For the Stuffing
2 hard-boiled eggs
75g (3oz) soft breadcrumbs
50g (2oz) suet

Seasoning
A little grated nutmeg
15ml (1 tbsp) chopped parsley
1 egg

To make the stuffing, chop the hard-boiled eggs and blend with the breadcrumbs, suet, seasoning, nutmeg and parsley, and bind with the egg. Put the stuffing into each of the pigeons, then cover the birds with the lard. If very young, roast in a hot oven for about 35 minutes at 200°C, 400°F, Gas Mark 6. Note that pigeons tend to have a fairly firm flesh and so it is better to roast for about 1¼ hours in a moderate oven 180°C, 350°F, Gas Mark 4. Baste the pigeons well during cooking or, if preferred, wrap each pigeon in foil after covering with lard and roast for about 1 hour 25 minutes at 180°C, 350°F, Gas Mark 4, opening the foil for the last 10-15 minutes.

This page: Jugged Hare (top) and Game Pie (bottom). Facing page: Roast Stuffed Pigeons (top right), Roast Pheasant (centre left) and Fricasée of Guinea Fowl (bottom right).

Duck with Orange Sauce

PREPARATION TIME: 30 minutes

COOKING TIME: 15 minutes per 450g (1lb) plus 15 minutes; 20 minutes for the sauce

1 duck

Orange Sauce
1 orange
150ml (¼ pint) water
300ml (½ pint) Espagnole sauce
15ml (1 tblsp) lemon juice
30ml (2 tblsp) port or claret

Place the duck in a roasting tin spread with fat or dripping. Season. Lightly cover the duck with foil or double greaseproof paper and place in the oven at 200°C, 400°F, Gas Mark 6. The duck should be basted frequently and the covering removed 20-30 minutes before the end of cooking time. After removing the covering, prick the breast all over to allow extra fat to run out and leave the breast crisp and succulent.

Orange Sauce
Pare the rind from the orange, discarding any white pith. Cut into wafer-thin strips and simmer these in water for about 10 minutes. Strain the Espagnole sauce, reheat with the orange rind, orange juice, lemon juice and wine. Serve the sauce with the cooked duck.

Mild Fruity Chicken Curry

PREPARATION TIME: 2 hours 30 minutes

COOKING TIME: 1 hour 15 minutes

150ml (5 fl oz) boiling water
150ml (5 fl oz) milk
100g (4oz) desiccated coconut
60ml (4 tblsp) oil
4 chicken pieces, skinned
30ml (2 tblsp) curry powder
25g (1oz) flour
300ml (½ pint) chicken stock
400g (14oz) tin pineapple chunks
15ml (1 tblsp) onion flakes
5ml (1 tsp) salt
30ml (2 tblsp) cream

Mix together the boiling water and milk in a bowl. Stir in the coconut and leave to infuse for about 2

hours. Strain liquid and discard the coconut. Heat half the oil in a large, heavy saucepan. Add the chicken pieces and fry until golden brown on all sides. Remove the chicken pieces from the pan with a slotted spoon. Heat the remaining oil in the pan. Stir the curry powder into the oil and fry for about ½ minute. Remove the pan from the heat and stir in the flour. Gradually stir in the stock, the strained coconut milk, the juice from the tin of pineapple and the onion flakes. Return the chicken to the pan with

the salt. Bring to the boil, stirring occasionally. Cover and simmer for 1 hour, stirring occasionally. Stir in the pineapple chunks and heat through, then remove from the heat and stir in the cream. Taste and adjust the seasoning and serve with boiled rice.

Roast Turkey Wings

PREPARATION TIME: 10 minutes

COOKING TIME: 20 minutes

Put turkey wings into a roasting tin, spread with fat or oil and season. Place in the oven at 180°C, 350°F, Gas Mark 4, for about 20 minutes, until the juice runs clear and the skin is golden brown. Serve with a mixed salad, if desired.

This page: Duck with Orange Sauce (top left), Roast Duck (top right) and Roast Turkey Wings (bottom). Facing page: Chicken Pie (top left), Roast Poussin (centre right) and Mild Fruity Chicken Curry (bottom).

Roast Duck

PREPARATION TIME: 10 minutes
COOKING TIME: 15 minutes per 450g (1lb) plus 15 minutes

Place the duck in a roasting tin, spread with fat or dripping and season. Lightly cover with foil or double greaseproof paper and place in the oven at 200°C, 400°F, Gas Mark 6. The duck should be basted frequently and the covering removed 20-30 minutes before the end of the cooking time. After removing the covering, prick the breast all over to allow extra fat to run out and leave the breast crisp and succulent. When the duck is cooked, transfer to a carving dish and serve.

Roast Poussin

PREPARATION TIME: 20 minutes
COOKING TIME: 30-40 minutes

2 poussins
1 packet sage and onion stuffing
A little fat

Make the stuffing as directed on the packet and stuff the birds. Place the poussins in a roasting tin with melted fat. Cook in the oven at 180°C, 350°F, Gas Mark 4, until tender.

Chicken Pie

PREPARATION TIME: 35 minutes
COOKING TIME: 45-50 minutes

450g (1lb) cooked chicken
50g (2oz) butter
50-100g (2-4oz) small mushrooms
50g (2oz) flour
300ml (½ pint) milk or 150ml (¼ pint) milk and 150ml (¼ pint) chicken stock
175g (6oz) shortcrust pastry
1 egg or milk to glaze

Cut the chicken into neat pieces. Heat half the butter and fry the mushrooms for a few minutes. Heat the other half of the butter, stir in the flour and cook for 2-3 minutes. Add the milk or milk and stock. Season. Bring to the boil and cook until thickened; add the chicken and mushrooms. Put into a 20cm (8 inch) pie plate. Cover with shortcrust pastry, brush with egg or milk. Bake at 200°C, 400°F, Gas Mark 5-6, for about 30 minutes or until the pastry is golden brown.

Chicken Liver Pâté

PREPARATION TIME: 30 minutes
COOKING TIME: 10 minutes

75g (3oz) butter
8 chicken livers
45ml (3 tblsp) cream
Good pinch of mixed herbs
Seasoning

Heat the butter in a frying pan and cook the livers gently until just tender. If you have an electric blender put them into this with the cream, herbs and seasoning. Switch on until smooth. Put into a buttered dish and allow to cool. When making a pâté by hand, rub the cooked livers through a sieve and then add the hot butter from the pan, cream, seasoning and herbs. Put into a buttered dish to cool.

Roast Chicken

PREPARATION TIME: 15 minutes
COOKING TIME: 15 minutes per 450g (1lb) plus 15 minutes

Place the chicken in a roasting tin, brush with melted fat or oil. Season. Lightly cover the bird with foil or double greaseproof paper. The chicken may be stuffed, if desired, but weigh it after stuffing to determine cooking time. Cook at 200°C, 400°F, Gas Mark 6. Baste the chicken frequently. Remove the covering for the last 20-30 minutes to allow skin to brown. When the chicken is cooked, place it on a carving dish and serve.

Turkey Cutlets with Lemon Sauce

PREPARATION TIME: 30 minutes
COOKING TIME: 20 minutes

6 turkey cutlets
Seasoning
30ml (2 tblsp) plain flour
2 thick rashers of back bacon
15g (½oz) butter
150ml (¼ pint) chicken stock
30ml (2 tblsp) lemon juice
30ml (2 tblsp) chopped parsley

Garnish
Lemon slices
Sprigs of parsley

Season flour and coat the turkey cutlets. De-rind the bacon and cut it into strips. Melt the butter in a frying pan and cook the bacon for 5 minutes. Add the turkey pieces and fry for 3-5 minutes on each side. Remove the turkey and bacon and place on a warm plate. Keep hot. Add any remaining seasoned flour to the pan and stir well with a wooden spoon, scraping the sediment from the bottom of the pan. Gradually add the stock and bring to the boil; simmer for 5 minutes. Remove the pan from the heat and stir in the lemon juice and chopped parsley. Taste and adjust seasoning. Pour the sauce over the turkey cutlets and garnish with lemon slices and parsley sprigs.

Turkey Cutlets with Lemon Sauce (top left), Chicken Liver Pâté (centre) and Roast Chicken (bottom left).

Index